MOVING WITHOUT SHAKING

The guide to expat life success
(from women to women)

Yelena Parker

First eBook Edition: April 2014

First paperback edition: April 2014

Moving Without Shaking Ltd
The Courtyard, 30 Worthing Road, Horsham
West Sussex, UK, RH12 1SL

ISBN: 9781632959430

For Martin Mackay, my partner and
the love of my life, whom I met on
my expat journey. You are the real reason
I chose country number 4...

Table of Contents

Chapter 1
Introduction

This book idea emerged in its final shape during a six-hour journey from Cambridge to Twickenham. Normally this adventure would have taken two hours, but snow took the UK by surprise, not unlike every previous winter since I had moved here.

I was reading Nassim Taleb's new book, *Antifragile: Things That Gain from Disorder*, and was drawn to his ideas about people, businesses, and economic systems having to be able to withstand shocks and evolve. It occurred to me that I knew quite a few people who have these amazing skills of restarting, absorbing shocks, and taking the next opportunity as it comes their way. My friends over the years always said how interesting they found my moves around the world and my ability to shake off roots and get on with it in a new place.

What is true is that I know quite a few people with the same ability. They pick up and leave for a better opportunity, a more exciting life, new friendships, new educational choices, or just to do something out of the ordinary, to get out of the routine. What's even more interesting is that most of them are women. There is a lot written, spoken, and conferenced about regarding the push that needs to happen to get women into better jobs, boards of directors, leadership positions in general, engineering and technology jobs, and any other areas dominated by men.

This book is about the "women next door" who have made some impressive moves abroad. We are not CEOs of large enterprises, Nobel laureates, politicians, PhDs, renowned authors, entrepreneurs who have made millions of (insert the currency), social media influencers, or celebrities of any sort, but that doesn't make our stories any less interesting. We have qualities that we all share and that make us successful at whatever we set our goals to achieve. I wanted to take a closer look at what these qualities are and find some key themes that might help other women pursue their dream international careers and lifestyles.

I pitched this idea at dinner in Oxford to a woman who had done exactly what I wanted to write about: she had picked up and left a small town in Poland, without any English language skills, and now was having an absolute native speaker level discussion with us about the benefits of this book. She said to me, "I would have really liked to have read it ten years ago when I was figuring out how to make my first move."

This conversation validated my concept. The book had to be written. There is a next generation of women out there asking themselves the same questions: "What do I need to do to leave my home country and explore life abroad? What if I don't have a lot of resources? Or even worse, what if I have no money at all? What if I don't succeed; it would be terrible to go back with nothing, wouldn't it? I am not in my twenties anymore; life gets more complicated; is it really worth it?" We all have been there, with our fears and doubts, looking at a large project and realizing that it would take a lot out of us to do it without anyone's support.

What makes me an expert on this topic of moving around the world and pursuing education or career dreams? I first moved from Ukraine to California back in 1999 to get my MBA. After several jobs with large technology companies in California, in 2008 I was very lucky to get an expat package and relocate to Switzerland for two years. Most recently, I moved to the UK and remain here for the time being. Having finished the Saïd Business School program in Strategy and Innovation at the University of Oxford and settled into a new job running commercial operations at a British software company, I apparently felt like an incredible amount of free time in the evenings was now available. So instead of catching up on sleep, I started pulling together this book concept. It suddenly moved to the status of a real project instead of just an idea. At the end of 2013 I quit my job, focused on finishing this book, and started an expat and executive coaching consultancy with the same name, "Moving Without Shaking."

In the past fifteen years since my first move, many people have told me that I should write a book because my life was so interesting. I completely disagreed. My perception always was that only very successful people, mostly monetarily successful people or media popular people, should tell their tales and write books. Then the e-publishing revolution happened. Then the social media exploded. Suddenly, a large amount of content became available to us instantaneously. Browsing countless blogs, tweets and LinkedIn profiles made me think that there was absolutely nothing wrong about putting your story out there for everyone to see. It's not just about the fact that I was told I should write these things down, it's also an opportunity to help someone who may be at a crossroad and needs a little push to take that first step. That's what makes our stories interesting — we relate to other people like us. There must be a woman out there trying to decide how to make her first move abroad right now. I hope to answer some of her questions.

I spoke about this concept with friends, many of whom also were my co-workers in the past or who are in my current circle of friendships that started in the office. They all loved it. And I mean, the feedback wasn't just, "Oh sure, it would be great." Many people, men and women, gave me very thoughtful comments and ideas about how I can approach this work.

Then came the idea of crowdsourcing the book. I can choose to be arrogant and believe that some of you would like to hear my thoughts on how to make your international relocation adventures a success. What would be more relevant is to find similarities in several people's stories and what they have determined to be the reasons for their achievements, their very own success factors, consciously selected for sharing with other international wanderers. On my journey I have been very lucky to meet many talented women who moved across continents, not just countries, and have gained great advantages in their careers and lifestyles by acquiring new cultural perspectives. Was it easy for them? Of course not. It's easier to write a book about it than actually do it. Have they all benefited from it? Absolutely.

I have reached out to a few of my female friends who had experiences with relocation abroad. Since we are all in different countries (surprise!), I resorted to email. Writing a small paragraph to sell the idea to them, including interview concepts and an invitation to participate, was surprisingly difficult. Then the responses came back all charged with emotion, excitement, and reminiscences about the past. I realized that all of us were so busy that we never had a chance to actually think through our moves and the energy that went into them as well as what they actually meant for our growth. The project was becoming much more personal and involved. Our very significant others got excited about it, some wanted to contribute, some said that it was an absolutely great idea. This support gave me the courage to formally launch into writing my first book.

And here it goes, my amalgamation and interpretation of nine women's views and experiences they acquired through moves across twelve countries, and their corporate career adventures. This book will attempt to explore not only their formulas for success in international moves but also address the most common fears of the movers. You are not alone! It's hard enough to move your flat or house within the borders of the same town. Understandably, when visas, planes, and shipping containers come into play, things get a lot messier. Don't worry, we know plenty of people who have done it, and so will you!

Why Shall I Bother Reading This?

All of us need inspiration. Some things that people find very simple are impossibly hard for others. My goal is to simplify your planning for your journey through different countries, cultures, jobs, educational programs, and relationships. Through sharing my own experiences and the stories of my friends who have done the same, I will offer you a few ideas for success in your international relocations and ways to do it without unnecessary stress.

Moving Without Shaking is about the roads that led us to new countries, new careers, and many new friendships. It's about "women next door" reaching their goals, but it's not just for women who are gearing up to make their first move.

Corporate executives who sponsor these moves should read this book, too. Even if these migrations are fully funded, not every move is a success. Money is not the only motivator for people who take on international assignments. They need support that stretches beyond the relocation agent and a contract covering the costs of the move, to be paid back if the candidate changes her mind in less than twelve months. What they need is a manager who understands what it takes, gets the uniqueness of the situation, and is able to step in to help. I have been there as a manager helping others with their moves and also received some mentoring advice myself. It was a rewarding experience and a reminder to not underestimate how much emotional investment these moves may involve for all the parties.

Another group of people who may benefit from browsing through a few chapters are students who are dreaming of or seriously planning to continue their education abroad. It seems simple: if you find your way to a foreign university, everything will come together in a magical way. One of my favorite films, *L'Auberge Espagnole* [Pot Luck], from the French director Cédric Klapisch, is about a group of students from all over Europe taking part in a foreign exchange program in Barcelona. The sequel, *Les Poupeés Russes* [The Russian Dolls], shows them settled into their careers and their respective countries five years later. What my book intends to help address is that time after graduation, the choices that we make right after that, and how those choices define the way our careers will evolve.

The hardest thing about writing your first book is coming up with a title. You feverishly search your brain for ideas, enter them into Google, and then pause before hitting "Enter." What if your title has been taken? *Moving Without Shaking* was an instant win. As soon as the concept was formed, I started wondering what the biggest fears I had to overcome along the way were going to be and whether things really were that scary. Then it occurred to me: it's about fearless women, moving, "expating," immigrating, vagabonding; all without any fears on the outside. What happens on the inside, the book will uncover. And there it was, moving without fear, *Moving Without Shaking.*

Successful International Moves = Transplants

It can be hard to see common traits if you don't have any "people who have done it" examples in front of you. Anyone can present him- or herself on the Internet as an adventurer, traveller, international entrepreneur, and wanderer but how do real people do it? I am talking about people who don't have huge amounts of money in the bank or any other form of assets, people who don't have a unique talent, who don't know how to start a business that pays the bills while they are travelling, or who are simply too shy to market their skills to get ahead financially.

I was always looking for role models even before I knew the term *role model.* It is definitely an American thing, something you learn when you start reading self-help books. In the days before the Internet, the only place to get inspiration was from people who you knew or who your friends knew. The truth is, before or after Internet crowdsourcing resources became available, there have always been people who are amazing at networking, with great ability to figure out many possibilities for getting introduced to the right people, and they do it over and over again until the desired results are achieved.

When I started researching the topic of international moves for people who pursue educational goals or fairly conventional corporate careers, I came across a lot of blogs about how to negotiate your expat package or how to find a networking expat community. What I was looking to find was someone else's experiences and why this person had made it as far as he or she had. Mashing all my friends' and colleagues' journeys together, I got a very eclectic mix of origination and destination countries: the United States, United Kingdom, France, Spain, Switzerland, South Africa, Russia, Ukraine, Poland, Colombia, Australia, and China.

What this book intends to do is to explore the building blocks of success in international relocations through the shared experiences of nine women who have done it. It's a puzzle that doesn't have to be completed. Sometimes a combination of a few pieces is enough to achieve that internal spark and connection with people around you that will help your next bold and certainly international move. Having more of these options will likely offer you a faster way to achieve the goal you seek. So what are the forces that create that perfect storm in a person's life to take his or her roots out and replant them in a new place?

Let's talk about the factors that have a major influence on whether your international move is going to be a success. I have found eight areas that contribute to how well adapted you are going to be to your move.

1. Education

To get started, it helps to have a formal degree. If you are reading this, you are probably not a twelve-year-old entrepreneur prodigy. Having completed your education basics helps land the right job that opens doors. Getting educated in multiple countries gives you a certain advantage over others in settling into an international career.

2. Fear of Settling

If you have a desire to keep on moving until things get even better, because you know they always will, you will find a way. Fear of settling pushes you to constantly be on the lookout. What if there is a better answer over those seas?

3. Languages

There is a lot to be said for learning English. It does open doors, countries, and educational opportunities. However, I will state the obvious: it's not the only business language. If you are an English speaker getting ready to go abroad, pick up another language or two, if not for the business setting, at least for the convenience of getting your hair done the way you want it.

4. Cultural Adaptation

Culture shock is not a myth. I have experienced it myself. The phrase sounds much worse than it really is but everyone will have her own adaptability threshold. The first move is always the most difficult one but the degree of difficulty varies depending on what your starting point is.

Reverse culture shock is also something you may come across upon your return home, temporary or long term. These are yet another set of feelings with which to discover how to cope!

5. Career Changes

Moves around the world often drive career changes. If you are looking to advance your career, take that offer to move. Interestingly, a high number of people who have taken the risk and moved then find that their current company offers no future prospects, or at least not immediate ones. Be ready for a move after your assignment is over.

6. Relationships

Among things that can put a strain on a relationship are moving together to a new country or leaving a person behind after the assignment is over. Being prepared and honest about your plans upfront is the best strategy.

Nobody likes surprises, and it doesn't matter who is driving the relocation idea forward. For both partners and friends, all your relationships will need to be managed differently. The most exciting part of all the opportunities is moving toward something and someone.

7. Networking

If you are close to your first move, you probably have some pretty strong networking skills. Networking skills are important at home; they will be even more critical once you cross the border. It's great that we now live in a world where staying connected is not an issue and building new networks is a breeze. The question is recognizing the need to put some real effort into it: online and offline.

8. Attitude

How much "stuff" does one person really need? If you have been hoarding things for years, the move will cause extra pain. Be prepared to leave things behind, sell them, put them into storage, and not think twice about them. Can you shrink your life into a couple of suitcases, at least for the first month after the move?

Do yourself a favor: don't listen to people who tell you that whatever you are planning to do is not going to work. There are so many things that can go wrong that you don't need to expand that list by listening to what people are saying who are choosing to stay in one place for the rest of their lives.

Knowing that there will be a Next Thing and that you will be seeking a Next Thing, your taking steps to make the Next Thing real is very important. There is life after your studies, your work assignment, or your long-term relocation move. It's up to you to plan for it or otherwise you may be disillusioned by the outcome.

What underpins all this is your ability to grow roots in a new place and, if you so choose, to do it over and over again. During your move and for a significant time thereafter, you will experience what gardeners call "transplant shock." Your immune system will be down, you will feel under the weather, and you will be sensitive to the new climate, temperature, and whatever other new conditions there are. It's a bit more complicated for humans than for plants, but you get the idea. Even though we are overconnected these days and can access anyone at any time on Skype, FaceTime, WhatsApp, Facebook, Twitter, LinkedIn, and many other tools and networks, our surroundings still matter. Your job may still include a lot of travel hours but it's important to feel good about your new living conditions, build new friendships, and get into your new adventure with your whole heart.

Chapter 2
Education

Men Come and Go: Education Stays With You

Last year I was having dinner with friends in Geneva, Switzerland. Their au pair, a nice teenage girl, invited her friend to join us. The conversation covered many topics and came to whether one should go to university or have a vocation. This topic has more to do with the Swiss education system setup than any individual preferences of the two girls. The au pair was having a great experience working part time, looking after fun children, and improving her French and English. Her first language was German. She grew up in a small village in the mountains and wasn't sure whether her next step would be to go to college or return to the village and find a nice boy to date and eventually marry.

Both girls were pretty, open-eyed, and happy. They liked socializing and clearly wanted to explore life. The move from a small village to the city of Geneva was for them what a move across the ocean would be for most of us. They were not offering any opinions but were just wondering what people do after the first twelve years of school. I wouldn't have picked up on the reluctance to go to university unless my friend pointed it out. Then I said what, in retrospect, was a very convincing line: "Girls: men come and go, education stays with you!" They giggled. I hoped they would remember it when they went back home, met nice village boys, and chose to have vocations, like cheese makers, instead of getting degrees in translation services.

There is absolutely nothing wrong with learning how to make cheese and spending the rest of your life doing it provided that it is what you enjoy. What I am talking about are options. Certain paths, quite often through formal university level education, open more doors for you than you could ever imagine.

Many people at the beginning of their careers may think that since they can read about anything on the Internet, they know about all the options they have in life. We all need help to make more informed decisions. Information quite often comes out in the school environment, perhaps not so much through classroom learning but through being around other people who contribute to learning.

I don't need to reach very far to find reasons to appreciate what formal educational institutions have to offer. This discussion is not about the quality of your degree; it's more about those interactions and meetings with your classmates, their families, their family friends, exchange program visitors, and, yes, sometimes even teachers, who give you a different perspective on what's important for your choices now and in the future. Sadly, we underestimate our teachers' contributions while we are in school.

My mom never went to college. After finishing high school she joined a local factory and remained there until she was asked to retire at the age of sixty-one. Her job involved no critical thinking, creativity, or opportunity to learn about the world outside the factory floor. She worked three shifts: four days on, then three days off, then on to the next round again. We barely ever talked until I was in my late teens. Mom would come home from work and go to sleep. In the late 1980s in the final throes of the Soviet Union's fight for survival, we started getting foreign TV, which was a huge improvement over the three officially approved channels transmitting two movies a day, two to three cartoons, a few hours of documentaries, and news carefully curated by the party. The soaps broadcasted were stories about oil magnates, slaves, wealthy plantation owners, movie stars, maids, and evil Mafia dons. Mom watched them all. Suddenly her world was full of knowledge about the imaginary lives of others. Did she want to have a different life? Try new things? She would never say. I know now that she likes when I take her shopping for things she never could afford before or once in a while offer her a trip to a foreign destination, an unthinkable idea when she was my age or younger.

While I was getting into university for the first time back in Ukraine, another young woman in China was looking for her first job. She studied English in college as part of her degree in Economics and International Trade and now was positioned to go into one of the state-owned enterprises, have a fantastic opportunity to live in Beijing, travel around the world, and contribute to building modernized China. The events at Tiananmen Square have tainted her college days, but people move on, societies bounce back, and so she graduated shortly thereafter and went on to explore her career.

Claire's parents were never home. They moved across the country to work long hours at a state-owned enterprise and left her growing up with grandparents. Claire's grandmother focused on education and on teaching Claire independence. Here is a bit of wisdom from a woman who grew up in "old" China, with a husband who was doing well: "It doesn't matter how good your husband's income is, you must have your own job. Even if your salary is low, you must work to be independent economically." Claire told me that years later all her hard work paid off and her grandmother was right. Getting into a prestigious university in Beijing was not an easy task, and obtaining that highly sought after degree in international trade was the only way to secure a stable and promising job in a state enterprise. That job took Claire all over the world as China was establishing import/export relationships in North America and Europe. The biggest reward came later when Claire, a single mother then, started working for American corporations, changed jobs, and made progress until she got to her dream move to Australia. We'll come back to her story later.

In the beginning of this chapter, I talked about education as something that stays with you while many variables will change: family, relationships, opportunities or the lack thereof. You may say, "Well, you have given us examples of communist societies. Businesses, state run or not, wouldn't hire people without a formal degree in those economies; everyone knows that! Plus this was years ago. Things must have changed."

I completely agree that there are people out there who are extremely entrepreneurial and talented. They will find a way to build businesses, turn them into empires, and live happily ever after. The purpose of this book is not to explore the "outliers," as Malcolm Gladwell would refer to them. We are compiling advice for those who are interested in getting pragmatic answers to two basic questions: (1) How do I build a successful corporate career? (2) What do I need to do to attempt this internationally (preferably working abroad at some point)?

Since I live in the UK now, I am always looking for interesting stories about people who became successful here. One of the most brilliant examples is that of Stephen Fear, who started his oven cleaning supply business in Bristol out of the phone booth at the age of fifteen and became a millionaire at age twenty. He didn't have a phone at home, so he figured out how to use a pay phone to receive calls, made the phone booth into his office, connected with American oven cleaning supply firms, and the rest is history. I enjoyed tremendously watching the video in which he tells his inspiring story.

Here is the truth: most of us are not like Stephen Fear. Growing up in Ukraine, I also didn't have a phone at home at the age of fifteen. So what did I do? I used my neighbor's line to chat with friends or used a dirty phone box on the corner, if it worked. I wasn't capable of using a communications line to help develop a business idea because I didn't have any! Ironically, years later, making friends with employees of a local Internet provider, getting access, and setting up an email account as soon as the first dial-up connection was available in Ukraine offered me a direct connection to people who helped me start on my international journey.

My advice to you is to get on with your college program! A high school equivalency degree is not enough to qualify you for an easy entry into the world of corporate careers. It doesn't matter what field you choose. One of my friends studied geography at Cambridge University. The connections she made there take a lifetime to acquire for some people. She now has a brilliant international marketing career, has moved from the UK to Switzerland, and successfully juggles her passion for marketing with her caring for and educating her three children.

The last time I checked, most companies are still looking for a college degree on your resume to bring you on board for roles beyond those of very basic administrative tasks. The more exciting the company, the higher the credentials they require. There are many companies, notorious for being interested only in candidates who attended elite schools. You can get great jobs through referrals, but having a formal degree in any field makes a better story of why you deserve to have the job.

In other words, it certainly won't hurt to have completed a program in any college anywhere in the world. In current times where we change our priorities, change our interests, and are no longer afraid to choose different career tracks, it doesn't matter whether you studied international trade or physics. You can build a career in any field. It's that first barrier to entry into the workforce that you need to overcome. In talking to many people around the world, I found that those who advanced in their careers without a college degree quite often felt stressed about it. What if have a degree became important? What if that one job that I really wanted to have was not attainable because all the other candidates competing for it had formal training? One sure way to remove those doubts and fears is to go for it. It doesn't matter how advanced you are in your career; if you feel that not having a formal education is holding you back, then choose a program, sign up, and get started!

Let's not get hung up on the quality of school you choose or the name of the school for your first college degree. Not everyone can afford to go to the likes of Stanford or can even test high enough to get in. The more advanced your credentials, the faster you will tend to move through your career steps, everything else being equal. If this is not a race but more of a journey for you, focus on studying what you can enjoy, build your college network, use it to get your first job, and the rest will come.

Formal or Informal: Education versus Learning Myth

Educational programs offer an opportunity for exploration. Choose a subject, get a list of recommended reading, and start. We often focus on the quality of our program, the fact that our teachers are theorists, not practitioners, and that we are so much better than they are. We probably are, by the way, but we need to define the criteria for success. Money alone is not going to do it. Most teachers will never have the income of a person who has chosen a commercial career. My personal favorite is to measure our ability to motivate before we judge. Can we be better motivators of people whose success in their personal and corporate lives we contribute to?

I hated writing essays. In fact, essay writing was the most challenging thing I ever had to tackle before college. Math was easy. English was manageable. But it was that time of staring at a blank sheet of paper, trying to compile my thoughts on topics about which I had no interest, that made me truly believe I could never write anything beyond three required paragraphs. Although I don't want to blame others, the highlight of my Russian literature class, which demanded writing essays, included my teacher screaming at the top of her lungs, "Scoundrels! Rotten souls! You will never understand Tolstoy!" I can understand her disappointment — none of us produced any work of genius during the five years we took literature under her watchful eye. I am certain that at the same time, somewhere in England, a disappointed public school teacher, without screaming, was saying in a dull and condescending tone to one of her pupils, "The only way I can describe your essay is subpar, Miss Parker."

Those who experienced Soviet-style education complain about the amount of memorization required and the lack of connection of theory to the real world. When I first met Jeff Fadiman, San Jose State University professor of global marketing who helped me get on track with my international moves, he vehemently complained about the amount of memorization required and undergraduate business students' inability to produce any original thought. His classes were inspiring. They challenged people and pushed them to get outside the boundaries of their conventional points of view. Students loved his classes and class discussions about different cultures and the world. The classes were also geography lessons for those who didn't bother paying attention to the rest of the world. Jeff is a huge believer in people knowing the geopolitical map of the region they are going to market to before they learn marketing techniques, not an unreasonable approach but often overlooked by many students and graduates who think of themselves as international business experts.

I think what Jeff got right was that it was easy to pick up principles of marketing from textbooks, which were available in abundance on campus. What he was offering us was a connection with people at a level that I am only now beginning to understand. His teaching was authentic, borrowed from his time spent studying and experiencing African cultures through living in Kenya, Uganda, Tanzania, Zimbabwe, Namibia, Botswana, Swaziland, and South Africa, and his travelling the continent extensively. Jeff's teachings went to the core of human interaction, to the grassroots, creating interest in each other and, thus, learning from real experiences across continents and across cultures. His emerging markets courses had a lasting impact on many generations of students.

Learning is something you never stop doing. It's your choice, unconstrained by programs and boundaries. Formal education is what helps you get that first job and start building your career. The unfortunate part is that learning about some subjects for your degree may not be very exciting. There are a lot of elements of the program you have chosen that you may not enjoy. Having spent a year doing academic advising in San Jose State University for business undergraduates, I can attest that many people are really clueless about what they are going to do after graduation. What they want is a list: Tell me what I have to do to graduate. What are the basic requirements? What are the specialist requirements? What if I have no idea what I want to specialize in? It's okay! It's a perfectly normal state of mind for any student. Think of it as buyer's remorse. You have invested in a big and probably very expensive thing (in this case your degree), but what if you have made a mistake? What if you started out fully intending to study art and then felt a sudden urge to become a finance manager? Relax! Education is a journey. The more you learn, the more doors open.

One thing I would caution against is investing all your energy into degrees and studies instead of trying to figure out if you are happy with your career track, unless, of course, you have elected to become an academic! If that is the case, disregard my advice completely. An entry into the academic world has never been among my ambitions.

No one grows up thinking, "I wish I could run operations in a mid-sized technology company offering cloud-based collaboration solutions." In fact, in college, this may sound like the last thing you would want to do. However, after you try a few career options, you may start figuring out what you are good at and what you are enjoying the most in a corporate environment. For some people, studying marketing principles is the most exciting thing on the planet. After getting their first job in marketing and spending endless hours on setting up marketing campaigns in two different systems accompanied by tedious data cleansing exercises to reconcile them, they realize that they would have been better off with a programming class that they insisted on skipping during their first academic advising session.

To maximize your formal education time, take those lists offered to you by teachers and program administrators and try to figure out what appeals to you. As with most things in life, you can't love every single aspect of every experience. Focus on things that will be useful and expand your college network. Professors are busy people. They will find time for you if you want their advice. Think of educators as people with whom you can practice your networking skills. Has your professor written a book? What is her favorite topic? Does he have a blog? Learn from them — maybe years later you will find that the topic is as important to you as ever.

The most common mistake we make when we first are in college is not engaging with the people teaching us. We are not bound to like every person who stands in front of us in the lecture hall. We don't necessarily become friends with every person who shares the classroom desk with us either, do we? What I suggest you do is to try to find a few points of personal interest and then identify the best people to help you further your education on those points.

L'Auberge Espagnole, or the Importance of Studying Abroad

Before *L'Auberge Espagnole*, there was my Russian Mafia, as I lovingly addressed them in my thoughts. They were four young Russian women from Ryasan, an industrial city near Moscow. They came to California to pursue MBA studies, sponsored by one of the generous churches from Menlo Park. I met them in 1999 when I first arrived on the campus of San Jose State University to start my business studies and work as Jeff's teaching assistant in a business writing course (Oh horror, remember, I hated essays!). They exuded curiosity, optimism, and ambition. We had endless conversations through the night, fueled by what I'd like to think of as moderate amounts of alcohol. We talked about career plans, success, seeing the world, and, of course, relationships.

I have stayed in touch with all of them after graduation. We maintain certain types of friendships throughout our lives regardless of where we live. That's how all my friendships are. My Russian Mafia members were not an exception — we are on schedule to see each other two to three times a year but most often in one-on-one meetings. Our schedules and locations are too complicated to get us all together at once, or maybe we just don't make the effort.

At the beginning of 2013, I sent emails to three of them to ask for help in researching this book. They answered me very quickly and passionately with statements of how good an idea this book was. If we inspired a few women to get the right education or take a higher career risk than they normally would, we would have succeeded. Incidentally, the interviews became a very thoughtful exercise as each participant had to spend some time to reflect on what corporate and life success meant to her and how she felt about her international moves.

So why go abroad to study? We all agreed that it's an enriching experience socially and culturally, and, if you come from a less developed economy, financially. Apart from learning the subject and formalizing your options to enter into a career of your choice, for many people, it's a once in a lifetime opportunity to get away from what they know, create new relationships and networks, and live in a melting pot, provided that you have chosen a melting pot kind of a school, of course. Watching *L'Auberge Espagnole* a year after our graduation made us all feel a little jealous. There they were, students in exotic Barcelona, right before the experience that we were going through. We had just left our fun international university environment and were thrown into our first corporate career explorations.

Strangely, we felt that Barcelona's environment and the Erasmus program was so much more glamorous than our California experience. Last year Ekaterina and I went to Barcelona together to take a long weekend break between my job in London and her business trip to Denmark. We wandered around the streets looking for a tapas bar still open at three in the morning and talking about how we couldn't have imagined being there back in 2002. We didn't mean just physically being in Barcelona so much as being there after ten years of experience in international business, technology, and world exploration.

The moral of this story, if there is one, is that we probably don't appreciate the value of the opportunities we have. If someone made a movie about us, a Ukrainian and four Russian girls meeting in California in the late nineties and seeking opportunities for better life experiences than we would have had in the post-Soviet landscape, that movie probably would look really glamorous to a couple of young women in Rwanda or Kazakhstan or almost any country in the world. I don't mean to reduce life to economic advancement alone or to suggest that only those who seek to get above the poverty level must go to school.

This is also a story of persistence and perseverance. We had no money. After four years of working at a university in the Ukraine, I had only $600 when I boarded my first international flight in Kiev taking me to Amsterdam, my connection for San Francisco. Julia had $200. The others didn't even care to remember how little they had. Ekaterina tried to apply to the highly competitive Edmund S. Muskie graduate study program and failed. The program was established in 1992, right after the Soviet Union fell apart. The goal of the program was to bring young leaders to the United States, give them an opportunity to study, and then engage them in a volunteer work before they returned to their home country. For the record, I failed to get admitted into the same program as well, and so did many of the people with whom I went to school for my university degree in linguistics, English, and literature. French I try not to mention; we'll get to that in Chapter 4. In retrospect, pursuing our goals on our own, without ties and commitments to a specific exchange program, was the best thing that could have happened to us.

A few years later, another young woman was boarding a flight in Bogota to take her to London through Miami. She failed to get a visa to the United

States to pursue her dream of studying business in an English-speaking country. She may not have gotten a visa because she was Colombian or because of plain bad luck, but there she was, taking a different turn, pursuing her master's degree in the United Kingdom, the Old World country that turned out to be less bureaucratic and friendlier to foreign students. We were talking about it as I was helping her arrange her first visa to the United States for a business trip. She was going to an event in San Jose as part of a global sales operations team that I ran at the time. She was still nervous about getting a visa, but this time she did.

Diana and I connected right away. We felt like our backgrounds were on the same track but in parallel universes: business education in English, study abroad, jobs during school days which were not intellectually rewarding but paid the bills, first serious opportunity at figuring out our career paths through a contracting job (not even a permanent employee contract), salary that paid the bare minimum to exist (in local currency, adjusted for inflation). What I saw in her was the same thing that Jeff saw in me: determination to make it and be a success, however success is defined; and the only people who should define that success were ourselves.

Recently, I met a driven young woman from Germany who came to the UK to study a few years ago. It was amazing to hear during a short lunch conversation how much more advanced she was in her thinking about her reasons for having gone abroad. She was looking for a diverse experience and wanted to broaden her horizons. She was so much more articulate than I ever was! She was not looking for an economic advantage. Simply put, the opportunity at home was fine but wasn't enough. She wanted more: experience, freedom, choices, meaningful education, and then a career. She is on a great track and is going to be a huge success in whatever path she chooses.

Let's get to the topic of resources. How are you going to fund your study abroad? Those who are fortunate to have family members to provide them with funds or who have managed to save up money can skip this part. Look for funding! Plain and simple. You have a huge advantage in reading this to inspire you, and you are able to access a wealth of fundraising opportunities on the Internet. I don't believe in spoon-feeding people, and this book is not meant to be a complete resources guide. Beyond Muskie and Erasmus, there are myriads of regional and global programs, funded by nonprofit organizations and by universities themselves. It's a huge amount of work to find one that is right for you. An alternative is finding a sponsor or a work–study opportunity that is not tied to a specific program and will not require you to compete with others. You can either pay your own way or have someone help you. Don't reject help if it comes your way.

Be straightforward with people about what you want. This advice applies to any situation. You don't need to be aggressive about it, just open. It helps to have a little charm or to stand out. People actually like that. Most of the lucrative twists and turns in my life and career came from sharing my goals or interests with people who happened to be in a position to help me. I don't just mean financial help. I credit Jeff with providing me with $68 for the entrance fee to get me into the MBA program. Everything else I paid for myself. Always.

The flourishing success of many crowdfunding organizations helping people raise money for anything from medical emergencies to gap year funding is very interesting. By the time this book is published, the list will most likely have evolved, but right now, IncitED and CrowdFundEDU look very promising. There is more information on Education Dive's site that you can find. All of these companies are an alternative to commercial fundraising sites and provide people with a platform to share their story, state their need, and raise money. I am not suggesting that all of you should focus on crowdfunding alone, but that is certainly one of many channels you can consider to raise funds for your education. For some people with a unique set of circumstances, the mob of benefactors may find such people appealing and may want to support them. These companies are taking the pain out of having to raise funds by approaching multiple people directly. Those who have a worthy cause and can articulate it will certainly benefit.

Executive Education: Network Effect

You have browsed through the first dozen pages of this book thinking, "College was so long ago that I can't even remember any of the benefits you are talking about." Well, I have something for you! Executive education programs are plentiful and the impact of them on your career and networking opportunities is tremendous.

People attend these programs for various reasons:

- To get an elite school on their resume to improve career prospects or simply satisfy their egos

- To meet like-minded executives and senior professionals for networking

- For personal development: never stop learning

- To learn from professors who are not only academics, but practice your trade

- To finally close an education gap by getting a shorter version of that MBA you never got

- For intellectual challenge

- To get better adjusted in a new country where your personal career or your significant other's career took you

- To go through a significant career change

- Work is paying for it. Why not?

- To party and make friends as if you are back in college for the first time (usually combined with one or more of the above)

Two years ago I was disappointed in how little advancement was available to ambitious people who worked in a large successful software company. Having tried to pursue a few new career opportunities to get out of the job I held to do bigger and better things, I found that I was stuck. Some people at this point exercise patience and try harder, network more, and generally wait until an opportunity comes along. My choice was to make myself busy with extracurricula activities until I figured out my next steps. In what now seems like a well-thought-out move I decided to apply to a Strategy and Innovation program at Saïd Business School.

To be honest, I am one of those people who always wished they had gone to a Big Name University. I was living in London, about to move to Reading, the least exciting place I have ever lived, but with one tangible benefit: it is thirty minutes by train from Oxford University. I have been to Oxford a few times and always had this thought: "I wish I studied here." There was something incredibly romantic about the spired buildings and the combination of hippy culture and elitist tradition. Without thinking about it for too long, I went with my favorite just-go-for-it principle, applied, and got accepted.

What did I discover? The quality of the curriculum is fantastic and really challenging. The faculty is international and experienced. We got introduced to Oxford tradition not just by studying but through a series of great dinners at the best colleges. Some of us, having gotten the taste of an Oxford diploma, went on to pursue an MBA. The best part for me was the network, consisting of very interesting, ambitious, and driven but also very down-to-earth people from all over the world.

I also was pleasantly surprised to find that the program had added the topic of women as an economic force and gender gap discussions to its set of lectures. Only 12% of the class attendees were women. I wondered why. We had a really diverse group of people in the class from every continent but Antarctica, yet women still were a minority. Is this ever going to change?

Let's face it: the program is quite expensive. If we look at it from a purely economic point of view, a lot of people attending this type of program get funding from the companies they work for while others are entrepreneurs and can afford it. To qualify, you have to be pretty senior in your work experience, not necessarily an executive but certainly a senior professional in your field. There are a lot fewer women than men who have both advanced their careers and reached the point of realizing that to go further they need to expand their network. Women have the additional issue of actually having to ask for and even push for sponsorship.

I hope some women who pick up this book will choose to participate in advanced programs around the world. Having women in such programs would really enrich them, such as the one I attended. Women participants would also be exposed to opportunities they never thought about before.

One word of caution: when signing up for an executive education program, have a conversation with the administrators about how much work is going to be required. There is a huge difference between a three-day refresher on leadership trends and a very committed series of four sessions stretching over four days each. There was a lot of reading material in between sessions and tests at the end! The graduation project was also not something to take lightly. You need to realistically evaluate your commitment of time to make the program a success. If you have a challenging job and family obligations, you can still do it! It will just require a lot of discipline and long nights reading Harvard Business School articles.

A quick benefit of this program was that I got more recruiters exhibiting interest in my LinkedIn profile, which led to an increase in my self-confidence, which led to more new opportunities, one of which I took the month after the program was over. At the same time, the program makes for a great conversation piece with people who also went to a Big Name University. If you felt like you were missing this connection, now you have it. Another curious fact in the UK is that a British citizen who went to a Big Name University some years ago most likely didn't even have to pay for it. So don't feel snobbed by people who think executive education is not good enough. You had to work hard to get it.

While I was enjoying my studies and struggling with the amount of work I had to do, I felt compelled to share my experiences with all my co-workers. Some of them listened politely but didn't show much interest. Others were surprised by yet another item I was adding to the long list of things I was doing. What I found most rewarding was that one of my team members became inspired by my stories and found an equivalent program in her local Stellenboch University in South Africa.

Education was never a priority at the beginning of Leeanne's career. She had to work really hard and look after two children at the same time. Now that both boys were going on to college themselves, she decided to take time and get a management degree, a short version of it. We discussed its value over and over again. She went for it, got accepted, and completed the program last year. Looking at her graduation picture I felt really excited about the change in her life and the self-confidence this learning experience had brought her. While this story is not about an international move, to be true to the topic of this book, there is potential here. Leeanne has been on a number of work-related trips abroad recently and is not ruling out a possibility that if the right job came along in California, she wouldn't say no. Having gotten a taste of school again, she is even considering a follow-up to the original program.

I have spoken to a few women from emerging markets (Russia, South Africa, Peru, Colombia) about the program. They are from different geographies, are on different paths, some still are in the homeland, while others have moved to London. One unifying factor for them was recognition of how Oxford's name on their CVs could change their lives, add more breadth to their experience, enrich them intellectually, and help them make connections. One challenge is that these programs are quite expensive. It's not that women don't want to study strategy! The challenge is a combination of location, financing, and how far in their careers they have gone so that they can believe the program is an achievable goal. During our graduation pre-dinner drinks at The Turf Tavern, an old pub offering an "education in intoxication," our academic program director said, "Why don't you start a scholarship fund for applicants from emerging markets?" There are many reasons why I wanted to write this book, and that thought added another good reason. Those of us who were lucky enough to seize an elite academic opportunity should team up to give back. I am not an expert in fundraising, but I am an expert in taking chances and moving my life and career internationally. Perhaps reading this book will get another woman from an emerging market to fulfill her dream of studying strategy and innovation.

We have looked at the value of education as a vehicle to increase your chances for having an international career and relocating abroad. What's in it for you? Besides acquiring the actual knowledge in a subject of your choice, you will get an opportunity to meet people, create future networks, and tick the box that some corporate careers will require. You also will learn how to manage freedom, be independent, and rely on yourself and your own choices: not your parents' or significant others'. The value of studying abroad is tremendous. All your experiences are enhanced, as if you have applied an Instagram filter to your life. An added benefit is having the ability to function in a foreign language environment, which will likely help with your first international work-related move. And finally, it is never too late to learn. Explore executive education programs to refresh your knowledge, get new points of view, and broaden your already well-developed network.

Chapter 3
Fear of Settling

The World Is Not Enough

The World Is Not Enough is one of my favorite James Bond titles, not the movie itself but certainly the title. I always think of it when a feeling of being stuck comes over me. There has to be more to our existence, our reality, than what we are dealing with. What if we push just a little harder? Can we get the world and more or whatever the world means to each of us?

I find that a fear of settling into the same job at the same salary in the same town in the same country, or (horror!) in the same relationship is what drives us to succeed in a new environment. Some of us just have a lot lower tolerance for routine. We find change thrilling, and even though it may be devastatingly terrifying we still go through with it. Change, risk, you name it: we will take it all! This embracing of change is not the same as having clearly defined goals.

I wish I could brag that from the age of seventeen I had mapped out a clear path toward degrees, careers, and countries. To be frank, I sort of fell into opportunities. In early 2013 I was having dinner with a British friend who I met while working in Switzerland. He is a very experienced IT consultant and worked in more countries than he cares to remember, as did his wife, who pursued a career in healthcare. He said something that I found really insightful: "Some people here in the UK would probably think of my career track as a failure. I didn't get a big consulting job after my MBA but sort of fell into IT consulting." What his career turned out to be was an amazing journey of fifteen plus years around the world on short- and long-term assignments. Like him, I didn't have a well-defined track, but I always had the sense that there were more things that I could be doing than I was already doing.

A combination of fear of settling and a love of change makes us take risks and leap into international moves voluntarily. Keeping options open is what seals the deal. I sometimes think in terms of what's left ahead. Not to be overly dramatic, but if you ask yourself a question of how many times you have an opportunity to do a certain thing you enjoy or dream about before your life runs out, that question really does push you to go for it. For example, now that I have made my first move abroad, will I ever be able to repeat it? How many times? Oh, I hope the answer is not "never!" It's not that my motto is to live each day to its fullest, but it's more about quantifying both the excitement and the routine and hoping to introduce an element of the unexpected into the journey to make it more interesting.

In terms of careers, fear of settling acts like an anti-routine agent. Long gone are the days when most people stayed in the same job for the duration of their professional lives. In fact, those of us who are recruiting people tend to be more suspicious when we see resumes showing no growth or change in responsibilities for many years. Will such a person actually adapt to a new job as well as someone who has changed jobs every couple of years, particularly if that person shows a track record of good career moves leading to growth opportunities?

Karen and I were introduced at a random meeting in our California office. Some time later after she became a catalyst for my move to Switzerland, Karen said, "We needed someone like you to help us with new ways of working in EMEA operations and problem solving. You made your goals to move to Europe known early on." I was surprised that my interest in driving change and my comfort with change were so evident even in a superficial internal business meeting. Never underestimate how you come across. If you have that fear of settling in you, it will make you truly an agent of change, not just for yourself but also for others. People will see this in you, and that is a great thing for changing positions and making your international moves happen.

Karen is even more accustomed to "moving without shaking" than I am. She grew up in Chicago but was always drawn to Seattle. She was already an experienced transplant before she relocated abroad for the first time. Her Chicago–Seattle–Silicon Valley itinerary was a strong indicator that settling was not something she knew a lot about. Karen became my role model for going after things you want and doing it internationally. Fear of settling pushes you to not compromise. If your job has run its course, you are not learning anything new from the experience, or the job is not attractive financially, change it!

People like Karen are my inspiration. I was absolutely honest when I said that I didn't have a well-defined plan for living in specific countries or getting specific jobs. Things aligned and the path shaped itself because I met people like Karen along the way. Learning about how she made choices, why she moved, how her career reshaped itself because of the relocations were the most insightful things I learned. While I don't apply the word *mentor* to her in my thoughts, it is absolutely what she is.

I started learning the ropes about successful moves abroad in times before the Internet intensified our ability to reach others. It was all about conversations and meeting people, and I continued on that path. Such encounters are really like pulling together a tribal history through long conversations and showing deep interest in what the other party has done. My academic mentor, Jeff, created the only existing written history of the people of Meru, Kenya. He has always been about storytelling, and this shows up in all his classes, books, and interactions with people. I have borrowed the idea from him that collecting stories and experiences to build your own is the best way to learn.

I hope this book will become an answer and a journey map for people who want to try this glorified international career path but don't have direct access to those who have been successful. Through the stories of these amazing women, I am sharing knowledge and our collective experience to help you make your own choice. What I particularly like about these women is that they represent very different backgrounds, countries, cultures, and lifestyles yet still have been able to achieve what many people would find stressful and just too hard to even plan. They have successfully uprooted themselves, replanted, and continue to flourish.

So is *your* world really enough? Alexandra grew up in a small village in Poland by the name of Bolejny. I gave up long time ago expecting people outside of the former Soviet Union to recognize the name of the city where I was born and spent more than half my life. It's a pretty big city, by the way, with close to a million people, multiple universities, and so on. When I booked a table in a brasserie in Reading, UK, to have a chat with Alexandra, I didn't quite realize how much more incredible her story was than mine. Bolejny has thirty-three houses with about one hundred residents. No one has heard of it. Remember my phone story? Well, Bolejny's only phone line was at the mayor's house. The rest of the houses got their phone lines when Alexandra was 18 years old.

Everything that Alexandra wanted to do was outside of the village. When she was thirteen, her parents took her to a bigger town nearby to learn German. Her parents were teachers. So her world was really small: she grew up with parents who, by default, were her educators. Why was she sitting across the table from me, telling me about her move to France, then to the UK and to the job that has her travelling to Morocco to project manage complex IT engagements? She couldn't imagine staying in her village for the rest of her life.

Her parents are happy people, intellectuals and educators. They are perfectly fine with their lifestyles. They occasionally travel abroad, and they are fully networked and connected: yes, the village not only has phones, but also a stable Internet connection now. What is a girl from a small village to do to see the world? Of course, get admitted to only the most competitive program in Gdansk to study telecommunications! Now we are talking about a big city move. One thing our childhoods had in common: not a lot of entertainment and the abundance of textbooks and classics. Having grown up in a family of teachers, Alexandra had no problem getting into a very competitive program where you had to beat nineteen people in math, physics, and German to get that twentieth seat. Education has certainly played its part in her future success but in talking to her, I could see that the idea of living in a small village and potentially working somewhere nearby, having a family, and settling down was never on her agenda. She had a travel bug and transplanted really well.

In my experience, once you have done it once, you can do it over and over again. The first time is the hardest, when you are tearing yourself away from everything you know, even for the sake of a new and exciting experience. The next thing for Alexandra was to improve her French and continue on in an exchange program at École Nationale Supérieure des Télécommunications in Bretagne. What helped was that Poland at that time expanded into a great relationship with Western Europe and exchange programs became plentiful. Her knowledge of French she describes as somewhere between conversational and intermediate by the time she was completing her program in Gdansk. While getting into a very competitive French school was quite a breeze, she did have to work hard during her first three months in France in order to follow the courses in French, understand the locals, and be able to converse with them.

Fear of settling came into play again when after a successful internship in Nice, she couldn't imagine taking a full-time job there after graduation. It was too small of a town! Her friends and family undoubtedly thought she was crazy. How wonderful would it be to live on the Mediterranean coast in a charming French city? Not for Alexandra. She could see why the retirees might enjoy that lifestyle but with IT career opportunities ahead of her, a choice to settle in a small town was not the one she was willing to make.

Let's come back to Diana's story and see how fear of settling played out in the choices she made early on. Her family lived in a small town called Buga in Colombia. She laughed as she said the name of the town. No one has heard of it. Of course not! The town was just a short forty five-minute trip away from Cali. When Diana graduated with a high school equivalence degree from the Colombian education system, she moved to Cali on her own. She was quite studious, so an opportunity to get into San Buenaventura University, a prestigious private school, was a perfect fit.

Diana made a conscious choice to move away from her family, share an accommodation with two friends, and spend five great years having fun, learning, and planning her next move. Forty-five minutes is not a long journey for any of us in most parts of the world, but what made a difference for Diana was that the move became her first decision to go out on her own. She probably could have stayed with her parents and commuted to school everyday. I certainly did! When I was seventeen and it was my time to choose a university, I was dreaming about Moscow Institute of International Relations but didn't have the guts to even explore it. So I chose a sure thing: the local provincial university, and stayed for most of the five years it took for my first degree at my parents' flat, living a low-key but familiar life. Instead, Diana jumped into a big unknown world. It's a really bold move for a sixteen-year-old girl who grew up with a great support system and without having to cook, clean, and generally look after herself! The feeling that her village was too small was always there. Minor inconveniences did not matter.

Diana has two brothers. In Colombian culture, she was a girl surrounded by confident macho men in the family. When she decided to attend a university in the UK, she told her siblings about the plan. They were concerned. They didn't want to be unsupportive but they talked among themselves about how little Diana was not going to survive. Years later, after Diana earned her masters in business in the UK and had worked for over seven years at American companies with a global footprint, as an EMEA sales operations lead, the brothers now say she is their hero and, frankly, the man in the family. Note that she doesn't perceive this as a derogatory term. Neither do I. It's a nod to tradition that has been turned upside down by a modern generation of women.

What I really like about Diana's story is how her world was getting smaller with every step she took, and she had to try new things. After graduating from university, she could have stayed in Cali. Many people remain near campus for the start of their careers after college. Her friends were not an exception. Diana, however, had to explore. Supported by her teachers and family she moved to Bogota. She started a marketing career but quickly realized that even a huge city like Bogota (by comparison) did not offer the level of adventure she was after.

The next step was Spain. She received further marketing specialization in Madrid. It was another fantastic step for her, expanding horizons, making friendships that will last a lifetime. The bigger goal was still in sight: London became that place where you don't settle but you continue exploring indefinitely. I listened to an abridged version of her story in a coffee shop in Covent Garden and could feel her passion and emotion in every word. It was such an amazing achievement to not give up and slowly put the puzzle together to reach the goal of becoming fluent in English and getting an international business career going.

By now you are probably thinking that I am only going to give examples of small-town girls becoming successful big city dwellers. Not at all! This process is not about the size of the place in which you grew up, it's about how much bigger you and your interests are than your familiar world. The most successful moves have a purpose. Travelling is what you do to change scenery. Relocation abroad is what you do to fulfill yourself.

Patience! Patience!

I dedicate this part of the chapter to something that I have very little of, as some friends would point out, which is patience. If you are always on the move, in your mind or in real life, can you actually be successful and achieve your goals? Do you need to stop, think, and plan like everyone else?

There are two distinct situations that I uncovered through the interviews. One is the need to exercise patience to get to the right place in your education, career, planning, relationships, experience, and many more meaningful elements of your life. The other is that people are constantly telling you to be patient. While I am not the most patient person you will ever meet, I recognize the positive effects of taking things step by step when it's productive to do so. On the other hand, it's important not to confuse this approach with external influences and with people who are constantly reminding you that you must wait. The former is making your journey happen, the latter is settling. The line is not so fine, really, but it's important to draw it. Depending on what career stage you are at, you may be too impressionable and may believe people around you who insist that you exercise patience. This attitude leads to not taking risks or taking risks that are too small to matter. To simplify, let's talk about good patience and bad patience.

When is it actually good for you to be patient? There is an old Russian saying: it took a while for Moscow to get built. To Moscow's credit, it's not over even now. Your career is a project, so treat it like one, with milestones.

Back in 2007, I was part of a sales operations team headed up by a really inspirational leader, the type of a person you always want to work with or for again and again. Brian was friendly, engaging, and super motivational. Anything was within reach. Unfortunately, the business was going down the divestiture track and he had to leave us, as organizational changes were already set in motion. However, I had the good fortune to spend 10 months in his organization.

Having never been a big planner, I had only a vague idea that I wanted to run things, manage, move, progress, get things done, and so on. Brian was the first person who in a ten-minute conversation changed the way I approached my career forever. You'd think by being an MBA graduate, relocating from Ukraine to California, changing a few jobs, and getting progressively more exciting roles I would have spent some time on reflecting what exactly I was after. I wish!

All right, I had a vision: becoming an executive in a global company. But even that I said out loud for the first time when Brian pushed me. He also drew a very simple chart on a piece of paper: career timeline, age. Who do you want to be? When is it going to happen? I have always been ambitious and impatient about the need to take the next step. What I didn't have was structure. Brian may have ruined me forever with that conversation. The visible timeline created a time bomb, like that tired concept of a biological clock. When is the time that you either have children or not? For me, the career timeline became a push and a pull at the same time.

I readily drew that line in the sand and said to myself that by the age of thirty five, I will be happy only if I had director-level responsibilities in operations at an international company. By age forty, I had to be a vice president or whatever title needed to be one of the people running the business. Not bad for someone who thought she might have been destined to teach English for the rest of her life at a provincial university in Ukraine (there is that fear of settling again). I still shudder when I imagine what my life would have been like had I not made my first move.

What I subsequently discovered is that Brian was one of a smaller group of corporate managers who were truly comfortable with the concept of other people having real personal goals, not necessarily aligned with the corporation's ones, and pushing hard to reach them. Many managers don't actually want to have that conversation or don't appreciate your "ambition" when talking to you. They probably are calling you pushy or aggressive behind your back. Here you get into the "bad patience" situation where people are telling you that you must wait. The worst thing about it is that those naysayers won't engage with you in planning. They just want you to hold on, wait, not move forward, go at their pace, and generally sit tight. And that is something really damaging for young minds as well as experienced corporate career warriors. Forget their pace. Set your own!

Diana inspired me to further describe good patience. You have to make a certain level of sacrifice to reach your goal. Some people get lucky quickly. I am a firm believer that hard work alone doesn't get you anywhere. You have to have a healthy dose of luck.

If you are not one of the people who are both super hardworking and super lucky and not an outlier on a long road of unparalleled success, pay attention! Let's say you don't have the skill set required or are perceived as not having the skill set or, worse yet, are lacking confidence to demonstrate your skills to others. In these cases, you will (oh, no!) have to exercise some patience. What helped Diana get through her first couple of years in the UK was a bigger goal and keeping her eye on that goal. Her English was decent but not absolutely fluent as it is now. She was in the UK on a student visa and had to study full time. She also did not have a lot of money to support herself. So in order to get through that period of her life, Diana took a job at Starbucks.

In short, here is a young woman with ambition, wanting to have a professional career in an international corporation, in marketing or sales, and wanting a good income. She already had one degree in business from her home country, Colombia, an exchange program certificate in marketing from Spain, and was finishing up her master's level of study in business in the UK. Diana already worked in marketing and taught marketing in her home country. The only job she was able to get in the UK was at a cash register at Starbucks! There is a networking lesson here, too, which we will talk about later; but seriously, how demoralizing is that experience? Talk about having to exercise patience.

One of the questions I asked when interviewing my international relocation role models was about the hardest things about their moves. For Diana, climate, language, and working in a meaningless job were the top three most difficult things about her move to the UK. The whole population of the British Isles wholeheartedly agrees about the weather. I agree and would rank the unfulfilling job experience as the number one hardest thing for those who haven't moved based on an expat package. Diana had enough patience to follow through to realize her dreams. She was very wise about it, too. She sold coffee and learned how to make it Starbucks style. Her takeaway was that you have to have a bit of humility if you don't have an extreme amount of luck.

Diana has a lot of friends from Colombia who moved abroad, including to the UK. They come to a foreign country, sometimes with a level of English that is far from perfect, and then get frustrated. Diana met a number of people who returned home because they could not adapt. They wanted to manage and run things but could not sell their skills in a foreign culture and in a foreign language environment. They poked around a little bit and then went back to their home country where they felt more appreciated and potentially got better career opportunities because they had "international experience." Diana did a coffee master class instead to match coffee with the right cake. In retrospect, she believed it was all a great learning experience. She persevered and got her first corporate job. She now feels great about continuously learning and about the progress she is making.

It's so important to be able to critically assess where you are versus where you should be and then make a plan to get there. The theme of returning home was a constant topic in the interviews. If you are relocating to run away from something instead of achieving your goals, the temptation to go back to where you started will always be there. I know this sounds like marriage advice, but there is a reason why. Relocation is just as disruptive to someone's reasonably comfortable lifestyle.

Not every relocation ends up being a permanent resettlement. Don't cut your international experience short if things don't go exactly the way you imagined them. Treating these low-qualification jobs as stepping stones and always focusing on what you are trying to achieve after you are done making ends meet are the attitudes that are going to take you places. Literally.

Speaking of making the ends meet, in the winter of 2002 I was unsuccessfully selling copiers. I used the Silicon Valley crash as an excuse but, more likely, I was just horrible at selling copiers. I could never get excited about the product. My good friend and San Jose State classmate, Julia, who I interviewed for this book, was actually simply amazing at it. She stuck to that path through the dotcom bubble burst and has been doing very well. I, on the other hand, was never meant to master that particular line of work.

My base salary was so low that I couldn't afford to replace the tires on my car — not a good thing even with California winters. When the highway patrol finally stopped me and told me that my tires were quite bald and I HAD to replace them, I realized sadly that I had to spend more money than I had. My debts were skyrocketing since I financed part of my

MBA and too many dinners and trips to breweries with my credit cards. So I did what I had to do: got multiple jobs. Freelance translation work was a little boring, didn't pay well, but at least gave me a false sense of achievement through working along the lines of my first degree, a job that I was expected to have before my move to the United States. The work was not terribly debilitating. The little assignments I got without putting a lot of effort into marketing myself were mostly related to marriage and divorce certificates. The feeling of setback was also strongly present as my interests were in the world of high tech, but suddenly my translation skills had to reemerge. In retrospect, I would have done anything to have that type of job when I lived in Ukraine, below the global standards of poverty. Things change when you gain experience.

This "good patience" conversation ties into the topic of education. The more education you have, the less happy you are, and I trust Eric Weiner on this one. In his book, *The Geography of Bliss*, he asserts that people with college degrees are happier than those without college degrees, while those who have advanced degrees are less happy than those with just a bachelor degree. I remember reading this and thinking, "Yes, that's so true." I felt so privileged when I was studying and also right after receiving my first degree in languages and literature. The path to a career was much more exciting and clear than my mother's. Nothing could stop me. I can't say the same thing about receiving my MBA. What causes unhappiness for highly educated and accomplished people? Their expectations are high, since they invested in themselves. They expect the world to recognize their achievements and immediately reward them with high-paying jobs, better titles, more responsibilities, personal fulfillment, and many other things that they imagine successful career moves entail. Unfortunately, it doesn't work the same way for everyone.

Many of us will often change jobs that pay the bills before we follow the things we love and do them well, thus achieving true success. Russell Crowe, in *Cinderella Man*, says one of my favorite lines in a movie: "I am grateful for the opportunity. I know that these days not everybody gets a second chance." I find this statement extremely insightful and not only in the context of second chances. Don't all of us know talented, brilliant people who have not maximized their potential? They didn't see a chance, were too scared to take it, or perhaps lived in a country where economic development never allowed them to become what they wanted to become. This is so much more often true of women, unfortunately.

Anyone can feel down if she invested energy and time in pursuing her goals and then the rewards don't come fast enough. Having resilience is key to success. My personal belief has always been that gender has nothing to do with our ability to grab hold of an opportunity. Yes, many studies have concluded that women need to be more assertive than men, and so on, but I think before any of us hit the glass ceiling, we simply need to go after things we need to do and not give up. I held three jobs at once to get a small boost in my income. It was that important to me. At the same time, I know plenty of people who have no interest in looking for extra income or finding a better-paying job — they are fine with their current opportunity and their pay. They want to have more but don't really feel it's worth the effort. We make different choices; there is nothing feminine or masculine about these choices if we live in an environment where no obvious hardships exist for women.

Lots of books about career building and, in particular, empowerment of women, teach you to grab opportunities, make choices, and take charge. I completely agree. You can probably tell from what you have already read that this is a shared belief of mine. In reality, careers crumble, lives change, sometimes for the better but other times for the worse, and we make tradeoffs. Not everyone gets the same chance. So keep on reading or just skip straight to the networking chapter if you are fully empowered to take your next step!

For those people whose professional aspirations have run into a wall, I will say that there is always hope that a chance will present itself, transform into an opportunity, and you will grab it. Just don't wait too long. In the meantime, do what has to be done to pay the bills. Quitting a job without having a next step in view works best for those who are financially secure.

Still stressed about not having enough money to cover my bills, and having unsuccessfully looked for other jobs, I desperately needed to make more income. Hiring of temporary workers for the Christmas season at all the major department stores was in full swing. All roads led to one of Macy's stores in Silicon Valley. They happily hired people without any retail experience in order to withstand the onslaught of Christmas shoppers.

It was a very strange experience, but looking back at it, the amount of learning for me from that job was unbelievable. Like Diana, I had to be humble and just focus on doing what was necessary while keeping my eye on my bigger goal of getting a job at a level that was inspiring. I discovered that I wasn't actually hopeless in sales after all. When the product met the need, I had no problem, like most sales people! Winter (even in Northern California) + coat sales = magic increase in sales skills for me. Selling coats to get a boost in income: what can be more unfulfilling for a freshly minted multilingual MBA graduate? I suppose not being able to get any job at all. I did get a job at Cisco before the next winter came around and wasn't forced to repeat the Christmas torture experience.

Pushing Eric Weiner's statement further, I would say people with advanced degrees are at a higher risk of being unhappy in the job they get after graduation if they were not certain about their career path before they went to school for the second time. This same pattern exists in relationships: getting out of a bad one and then getting together with someone else right away frequently does not work out. It's really not much different for career choices. Why would it be? You have a high level of emotional commitment to a long-term job. Then you embark on a journey to better your education and, subsequently, your career options, but what you find when you graduate is that there is no ready-made solution waiting for you.

If getting an advanced degree is about escaping existing job options as much as it is about learning, let's acknowledge that. We have to spend time networking and figuring out what it is that we want from our career changes while we are still in the safety of the classroom. Once we are out, we are out, rushing to get the next great gig.

Quite often people spend five to ten years with the same company, get out, and can't hold the next job for more than six to twelve months. Sometimes it takes a few tries to get the next job going. Again, don't get me wrong: I am a believer in making quick changes and realize that quick career shifts today are completely normal and expected. However, settling is not going to get us closer to our goals. Let's not jump into the first thing that becomes available but instead spend some time charting the pros and cons of a job choice and understanding how taking the next job fits into our overall life and career plans.

Natural Curiosity as Natural Selection

In interviewing people for this book I was looking for patterns. What is the main driver for someone to be able to commit to an international relocation or even to consciously transplant him- or herself with the goal of fully growing roots abroad? Fear of settling is not what everyone easily relates to. I strongly identify with it, both in my personal and business life, evidenced by the fact that I had three not particularly successful marriages and couldn't imagine working for the same company for twenty years, despite all the good stuff that a large American multinational company could and did offer me.

All the women I spoke with couldn't be more different in their motivations to take their personal leaps of faith to move abroad. Some moved to escape from an unfulfilling lifestyle and to explore (yours truly included). Claire could never understand friends looking for a better life abroad. Her life was perfectly fine, according to the standards she wanted and that she built for herself. Her move to Australia from China was to explore her own opportunity, to make it bigger, and at the same time, to give her son exposure to a foreign culture. Diana wanted to master English — it didn't matter in which country: the United States, the United Kingdom, or even Australia. She subsequently wanted to have a better opportunity when she returned to Colombia.

Olga, Ekaterina, and Julia all made their first move from Russia to California to get their MBAs. They didn't have a master plan for where they were going to end up once that first goal was reached. I spoke with Olga on Skype about her last move. Why Ukraine? Why Odessa? Well, guess what? Our interests and priorities shift as we gain more experience. Fast-paced corporate life in Moscow turned into dread and a rat race. The weather and traffic were absolutely awful. After a short stint in the UK, she started seriously thinking about whether the big corporate thing or even working for other people's businesses was right for her. As a result, the move to Odessa was great for her in terms of an experiment in entrepreneurship and a chance to live in a much better climate again. It also gives me a fantastic excuse to come to Odessa a couple of times during the summer every year. I would go anywhere to see my friend, but I love the town as well, so it's a winning combination.

I looked deeper for patterns. Was there something in our childhood experiences that made us more risk takers? Or was it our personality types? Would extroverts be more successful than introverts in taking on a foreign assignment? I am sure that if I did a quantitative study, I would have gotten a lot of really big data and been able to crunch the numbers, while completely missing the point. We get so excited about numbers and their interpretation that people's will to just get on with it and do it gets mired in statistics. What I wanted to do is to confirm my own intuition that our behavior is a combination of natural qualities and taking advantage of opportunities. International relocation comes with a price but it also comes with lots of benefits. Single, married, and divorced people move; careerists and entrepreneurs move; people who travelled and moved a lot with their parents and those who always lived in the same place move;

overachievers and people who prefer a balanced lifestyle move.

As the interviews went on, the pattern that was easily distinguished was not so much a list of specific reasons or profiles of people for whom the moves made sense, but an interesting choice of adjectives and phrases that they used to describe their decisions. If I created an infographic, the word *CURIOUS* would be in the largest font, straight in the middle of the page. I stumbled upon the topic of natural curiosity.

All these women were curious, wanted to explore, experience, understand, experiment, learn, figure out, take a chance, give it a go, and try it out. If you are a curious person with an open mind, living abroad is something that you will likely find very rewarding. There is nothing like cultural and linguistic immersion to satisfy that curiosity that you had as a child when you stared at geographic maps. Certainly cultural immersion adds some color to the changes that those maps have since then undergone.

Sure, it's much easier for those who have a social butterfly personality to get adjusted and to satisfy their curiosity through tapping into many local groups and friendships. By all means, it's easier to move without a family. Whatever your personal situation is, there will be some challenges that you will have to overcome. Curiosity doesn't kill you; it continues pushing you forward through hurdles and challenges.

Chapter 4

Languages

Languages in Business and Life

My grandmother, Nadya, chose my first school out of fear that I would not have enough to do if I went to a regular neighborhood school with a standard curriculum. In the 1980s, every Soviet city had a few schools in a particular district that offered extensive studies in certain subjects, usually languages, math, or chemistry. Extensive studies basically meant minimally an extra two hours a day in school and a much larger amount of homework compared to my friends. At that time education was free and children were assigned to a school based on the proximity of their parents' address to the school. Today these types of schools have acquired the status of lyceums and other fancy names but the basis for them remains the same. The main difference is that there is a price of admission.

Since I was reading all sorts of things from the age of four (mostly fairy tales and Soviet propaganda) and doing a fair amount of math at age five, my grandmother was concerned that while everyone else was learning how to read and calculate, I would be wasting my time and becoming lazy. This is how random luck worked. The choice of study for me could have been anything, including chemistry, which would have been awful. Instead, the school my grandmother chose offered a specialization in English. Did it make a difference? By all means! I am not a natural linguist. Believe me, my French, which I took in college, didn't come easy and is really far from a business conversation level for me. Because of the extra ten years I spent studying it, English is truly my first language today. In fact, it takes a little bit of effort to switch back into my native Russian. I generally prefer English — it feels more action driven.

I love Malcolm Gladwell's concept of 10,000 hours from his book *Outliers.* He asserts that if you practice anything for this much time, you become an expert. I reckon my investment into English studies in the ten years it took to get from elementary school through high school equivalence in the United States was about 6,000 hours. Adding a college degree with the same specialization on top of that definitely did the trick. It wasn't brilliance or a natural talent but rather a consistent investment of time and effort.

Now, has this investment paid off? Absolutely! It's impossible to feel like you are a citizen of the world without speaking English today. It is also impractical to imagine that you can have a successful international career without a level of English as close to native fluency as possible. If you are reading this book and are thinking, "What do I care? I already speak English," hear me out first! English is only one part of the languages journey.

Having moved to the UK at the end of 2010, I started establishing local networks, paying more attention to local news, and stumbled upon some stats on the decline of general interest in foreign languages by pupils who attend British state schools. Private schools are still able to keep the demand and interest up. Public opinion as reflected in newspaper articles seems to be that since languages became a voluntary option in 2004 for pupils over the age of 14, the country's educators could not stop this slide. Now the country is facing an "alarming shortage" of people with foreign language skills.

Most of my friends in Ukraine who went to state schools with no specialization in the 1980s had a similar experience to that of modern British kids. They gave up on languages after a couple of years of unsuccessful study. What I find fascinating is that now that national borders have opened up and learning a language gives an average white collar worker in Ukraine an economic advantage and better career opportunities, a lot more people are finding a way to learn English, primarily through private lessons.

Nowadays, children in Britain are not planning very far in advance and don't have the same economic pressures as in Ukraine; besides, they already speak English. Teachers are trying to reignite interest in foreign language studies through workshops, seminars, and career fairs. A few schools in the Reading area organize an annual event where they invite several multinational companies to talk to students about the importance of learning foreign languages and the impact that this can have on their careers. In 2012, the event was hosted at Wellington College and I was recruited to give a closing speech on how languages helped me in my career.

Let me put my English skills in perspective. I still speak English with an accent. People always tell me that it's charming and unique, but at times I hate the fact that I am always "not from around here." Then again, that's what living in the global village really means. You are never from around here but you are comfortable with being anywhere.

Having arrived at very the posh premises of Wellington College, I was a bit nervous in thinking about what example I was trying to present in my speech. I am a foreigner who had to learn English to succeed in the international business scene or, frankly, to even have a shot at entering it. These kids already had an advantage! Cecil Rhodes' famous quote about being British means you have won the lottery of life doesn't quite ring true in 2013 but still, there are some clear advantages. "The Where-to-be-Born Index, 2013," published by *The Economist*, puts the UK at a comfortable 27th place and Ukraine at 78th, right above Kenya and Nigeria. With Switzerland at the number 1 ranking, it makes sense why I felt so happy when I was living there.

What did I have to do to offer a compelling argument as to why languages were still important? I focused on three things: keeping an open mind about your career, language as a communication and culture exploration tool, and language as a means of building trust. I used some personal examples to back up my story. The result was surprising. One of my colleagues, originally from Russia, was really moved and told me that she identified with my story. The audience, however, was dead silent. I still don't know whether the talk was a good thing or not. The teachers came up afterward and said it was exactly what they were looking for.

When the idea for this book took shape, I wanted to come back to these three topics around language study and explore how languages shaped my friends' and colleagues' choices. I think back to San Jose State University and my Russian friends' stories. We all had the same background— languages and literature. We grew up in a world where career choices were limited and education really mattered to the point that once you picked your field of study, there was not very much wiggle room. We were generally expected to teach English at some moderately respectable institution or translate. A provincial university in Russia and a provincial university in Ukraine held approximately the same value.

What we didn't know was that the walls would suddenly come down and an influx of foreign investors, academics, and business people who spoke no Russian or Ukrainian would create a brave new world of opportunity for those of us who spoke even mediocre English. As I was graduating from university as an English major and a French minor (which remained quite minor), I was approached by one of our deans to come on board and teach at my alma mater. The university created a management faculty and was looking for teachers who would deliver English courses with business themes. I knew nothing about business, contracts, or any such thing but immediately jumped on the opportunity. I spent four amazing years learning and teaching at the same time and got an opportunity to translate for an American nonprofit organization specializing in delivering short business courses in emerging markets. Coming back to my theme of keeping an open mind about your career, it was then, at the age of twenty five, that I realized that teaching was really not going to be it for me. I got the business bug! I moved to California to study for my MBA.

When I think about Alexandra's path, it's clear that the road to her wide spectrum of opportunities was paved by language learning. Polish was not going to be the cornerstone for her career building. German was a prerequisite to get into a prestigious university in Poland. French opened the door to an exchange program in France. When it came time for her to pick a career, even basic English helped with her move to the UK and multiple job choices. Was English the most important of them all? Well, it really depends on what you are trying to achieve. If Alexandra wanted to take jobs in France, her basic English would have been enough. She couldn't really settle in a nice Mediterranean city and was after a faster-moving lifestyle and a broader international business opportunity. This goal made her acceleration of English learning mandatory. It wasn't so much a large amount of planning but rather keeping an open mind about languages, countries, and opportunities that made many of her achievements possible.

Diana's interest in learning English and adding a foreign language to her tool set drove her to make a decision to study abroad. She had already made a career choice to get into business and work in marketing but felt that her Colombian experience was not going to be enough. In our conversation, I discovered that her destination for continuing her business education didn't really matter as long as the country was English speaking. What I am happy about is that she ended up in the UK since this is where our paths crossed. Her parents were thrilled that she didn't pursue Australia — the perception is that Australia is just too far away from everywhere else. Her American visa problem was a shame. I really hope that one day we will see fewer government barriers for people like Diana whose intentions are to learn and to be truly productive global citizens. Diana kept an open mind about her career all the way through the journey. Once her English level reached the level she wanted, her desire to return back to Colombia diminished. Language and education have become her competitive advantages and have opened her path for broader decisions about what she wanted to do in business.

Language as a communication and culture exploration tool for me personally was a huge discovery. Ignorance really is a blissful thing. Living in a country where the majority of people didn't speak English, I felt like I had a unique skill. Boldly, I thought that my command of English was at the highest standard possible. Okay, it was pretty decent. Only after I arrived in the United States did I realize how much more I had to learn. One of the most important lessons to be learned, not necessarily a linguistic one, is once you land in a country where the majority of the population speaks the language that used to be your competitive advantage in your native country, the advantage part is completely wiped out.

Julia put it very well. One of the most shocking things for her in the United States was that little kids spoke English. And their level of English was better than hers! It's not quite true, of course, but you get the point. Language is part of your cultural experience. We didn't particularly notice living in the ruins of the Soviet Union how homogeneous our culture was, both in terms of national identity and language. There weren't a lot of tourists coming through the sleepy streets of industrial cities like Ryazan. Just a few years ago, returning to one of the Ukrainian cities with a couple of friends, I was walking through an area where a few street urchin types were drinking beer. They actually mocked us, screaming out some obscenities about Americans. I was speaking English, so I couldn't tell whether they recognized me as a local and were screaming to insult me for being with foreigners or were simply amusing themselves because they saw foreigners who wouldn't understand them.

I was interviewing Julia about languages and how her life turned out after she moved from multilingual California to Colorado. There is a lot to be said about culture shock and I have a whole chapter coming up about it. One thing that came out of our interview is a reminder that xenophobia is still a universal trait. You run into it in Ukrainian streets or on the phone in Colorado. Julia speaks perfect English, with a mix of Russian and American accents. No one has a problem understanding her. She expresses herself clearly and is quite charming and funny when she speaks English. She moved to Colorado on a whim to get away from the high speed of life in California and to enjoy the mountains and the mellow lifestyle. Julia and her husband went on holiday to Montana and were so charmed by a very different lifestyle that upon their return they looked at a map of the United States with the sole purpose of finding a place that still offered an opportunity to have a job in technology but was not as stressful as the Valley can be.

Julia is amazing at sales so she had no problem finding a new job and, within a couple of months, they packed and left for Colorado. She had a few interesting positions there, all in the world of copier sales, and clients liked her. The only example that she cites as a major cultural difference and something that would have never happened in California is a phone call that she made to a small local law firm. The customer had some issues so she called to help resolve them. Julia always puts customer service in the forefront of everything she does in sales. Too many people in her industry love getting a sale and never looking back. She believes in creating lasting relationships and being memorable, in a good way. This particular customer was dissatisfied with the service. The reasons for this lawyer's extreme misery don't really matter. What matters is that he chose to respond to Julia's phone call and an offer to help by saying, "Call me when you learn how to speak English." Street urchins and lawyers alike can be xenophobic. Let's not dwell on these examples. Just be aware, we still live in a world where being different from what people are used to may generate odd reactions. Deal with it!

I asked Julia if she ever wanted to take a course that would make her sound American, with a sort of neutral news anchor accent to help her blend in. Those ideas certainly crossed my mind when I was in the earlier stages of my career. The things we imagine would make a difference! Julia's response was, "My accent is what makes me stand out. I celebrate it because it's part of what makes me special. Why would I want to blend in?" She left California for Colorado without much thinking about coming back. After three years in Colorado it became obvious that California was the place where she left her heart. One thing that she was wondering about was whether the customers she left in California together with her heart would remember her. They did! She changed jobs, left the state, came back, and people who knew her ten years before still remembered her. You are the Russian lady who helped me! I really liked dealing with you! You were different. I remember you.

At the Symantec cosponsored languages day for British students hosted at Wellington College, I talked about language as a communication and culture exploration tool and quoted Eric Weiner and his concept of going native. I am not really original. All great concepts of a remotely philosophical quality have already been thought of and explained by much cleverer people. It is great to relate to these ideas when you are lucky to have had an opportunity to live them. Eric Weiner talks about those migrants who immerse themselves so deeply into a local culture that the only way to describe their experience is to say that they have gone native.

I have absolutely gone native in California. Once I graduated, I felt exactly like any other American business degree graduate — I was trying to have a business career in my now *native* language, English. At the age of twenty seven, I no longer felt that speaking a foreign language was an advantage. It wasn't foreign anymore; everyone spoke it! I didn't think much about how the tables had turned and that being a Russian speaker could have given me a competitive advantage. I was in my second year when a new classmate asked me whether my accent was Russian. Once we established that I had grown up bilingual, Russian and Ukrainian, before going native in California, she asked me if I wanted to join the company where she worked to do some software testing in Russian.

I had no software testing skills or interest in a quality assurance engineering career whatsoever but was flattered that my language skills could come in handy, so I agreed. I quickly realized that my language skills could be put to even better use since at that time software development outsourcing to Russia and Ukraine was on the rise. Living in the United States had also taught me that you had to be proactive. If you wanted something, you had to go after it. And so I went. I approached our vice president of engineering and offered to research suitable Ukrainian software development firms. This action yielded real experience for me in searching for a vendor in two languages, negotiating pricing, and going on my first business trip abroad, all expenses paid, to my former home country.

Interests and careers change. Sometimes the change happens very quickly and unpredictably. Through some fantastic turns, in a couple of years I landed a job at Cisco Systems as a Leasing Services Manager.

There were about thirty of us in the same type of function. How do you differentiate yourself? Believe it or not, a foreign language played somewhat of a role. I wouldn't say that language is the only key to success; you have to want to take a chance, to do something new, and, of course, to be a bit lucky. I mentioned earlier that I minored in French at a Ukrainian university. You don't always have to be fluent to get tangible results in a business setting. Sometimes basic or intermediate knowledge can do the trick.

In the operations group that I joined at Cisco, everyone was supporting the U.S. territory while Canada was outsourced to a service provider in Toronto. We didn't have any French speakers employed in California to deal with the French part of Canada. Being able to read contracts and invoices in French was useful and was part of my pitch to land an opportunity to become a team lead and then progress into a management role in operations, running a team covering major parts of the United States and Canada. It does take some adjustment to realize that learning a foreign language was actually not a goal in itself but a means to reach a bigger goal.

In the dark auditorium at Wellington College, I mentioned the third theme: language as a means of building trust. This theme goes against the examples of xenophobia you read earlier. Well, I do believe that people are naturally more interested in building trust and understanding each other's motives than completely shutting each other off, particularly if you are on a business assignment and are surrounded by educated people rather than in the middle of nowhere being harassed by narrow-minded strangers. It really pays to speak more languages than English when you are in just about any country in continental Europe.

After four years at Cisco, I was recruited by VeriSign. At that time, VeriSign was a Silicon Valley company famous for operating the infrastructure for major Internet domains and security. This job was a big change for me. I had become used to being a part of a very large company, and I didn't really need to explain what Cisco did. The VeriSign opportunity felt risky. It's ironic because the company was actually pretty big — with $2 billion of annual revenue, it was a really stable business. It's not like I was jumping straight into entrepreneurship or taking a pay cut. On the contrary, VeriSign's offer was very generous and held a lot of promise for career development. My discovery was that suddenly I had a lot more exposure to major areas of the business and felt like what I was working on everyday was actually making a difference. After a year and a half of running a sales operations team at VeriSign in California, I was approached by the European management team and offered a job in Geneva, Switzerland to run a couple of back office functions, credit and order management, in addition to my sales operations team. This is where the story moves toward building trust. What I mean by using a foreign language to build trust is an added benefit of cultural exploration. When I moved to Switzerland, I discovered that a few of my new team members as well as other people in the office were "frontaliers," French residents, commuting across the border to work in Geneva, the French-speaking part of Switzerland.

We established that my French was not fluent, but sometimes trying is what counts. Can you work in Geneva without speaking a word of French? Absolutely! It is one of the few cities in the world where expats can stay in their English-speaking bubble and not worry about learning the local culture, let alone trying to speak French. Is it rewarding to try to improve? Without a doubt! While your colleagues are always going to speak English with you during coffee breaks, it feels a lot less awkward to approach a group and not have to make everyone adapt to your language choice. I have made some great friendships and learned a lot about French and Swiss culture during my two years' assignment in Switzerland.

In the spring of 2013, I flew to Seattle to interview Karen for this book and reminisce about our great times in Geneva. Sitting in one of the independent coffee shops that the city is famous for, not just Starbucks, I was typing away to keep track of the story. The emotion of it, though, was much more important. We became friends during our expat assignments, made friends with locals, and worked on building trust with people and departments they represented. Karen was really well-travelled. Her relocation experience within the United States was vast. Her move to South Africa was quite adventurous. In all of those moves, she never needed to excel at a foreign language. Coming to Geneva changed that. She admitted that learning French was not critical to her business experience in Switzerland but really important for building relationships. I agreed, since we both held internally facing jobs. We didn't have to speak to customers and partners throughout Europe on a daily basis. Our sales people as well as a few members on our team were easily able to cover five to seven European languages and Swiss versions of French and German along with them. However, learning a local language was really beneficial for our social experiences. For instance, it is much more convenient to be able to speak to your hairdresser rather than try to gesticulate to him or her what your expectations are. Karen pointed out that her local friends and colleagues really appreciated her trying to improve her French and encouraged her.

Claire and I got on Skype early in 2013 to talk about her international experiences and languages. I was fascinated with languages' impact on her life and how well her experience fit into trust building. Growing up in China, she was exposed to multiple local dialects. Claire's parents met in Xinjiang where her dad moved at the call of the government. Job opportunities were better but did not translate into any major jobs. The overall lifestyle and standard of living were not great and education standards were lower, so Claire's parents sent her back to Suzhou to live with her grandparents and go to a better school.

Claire grew up speaking Mandarin but she also was fluent in the Suzhou dialect, which is very similar to Shanghainese, so she got the benefit of understanding both. Claire's take was that people liked when you were from their hometown. It was easier for people to trust you. When she joined the business world, this benefit became even more transparent. Usually people who were raised in Shanghai spoke Mandarin with an accent. Claire went to the university in Beijing, so she sounded like she was from Beijing and fit in. Then again, sometimes in the middle of meetings, people from Shanghai would switch to their dialect to exchange a few semiconfidential opinions, but Claire still could understand them. She usually would acknowledge that she understood, earned a bit more respect, and got more opportunities due to her trust and understanding.

Similarly, now that I am past the stage of trying to use the Russian language to my advantage, it has become an advantage. I get very close quickly with other Russian speakers who work in the same company or whom I meet in various business settings, in any country. The encounter doesn't have to be in a meeting in Ukraine or Russia. This language skill helps form new productive business relationships faster and create trust. The conversations are, indeed, more open, even emotional and heart felt sometimes. Going back to Ukraine to talk about outsourcing opportunities is also super easy. Now that I have both business experience and a language edge, it's so much faster to cut through the noise and address any questions head on.

What I have learned from Claire's languages story is that even within a country that is far from being homogeneous, spending time and effort on learning multiple dialects can bring you that extra edge to your career. English language studies, of course, were critical to Claire's future and, ultimately, career building and move to Australia. Majoring in international business meant entering a career that involved communications internationally, with

English being the key language. Claire considered herself lucky for being born at the right time when more opportunities opened up in China, having an opportunity to go to college, and making the right choices. Her family clearly had contributed to her path. Her grandmother studied English at school and it wasn't a surprise that Claire continued on the path of learning. After graduation she joined one of the large state-owned export–import companies in China. Claire couldn't expect to get a project management position or a management role right after graduation. All young grads were starting in various assistantships that involved translation from Mandarin into English to some degree. This work was a great training ground to prepare for project management that had to be done completely in English.

Claire has lived in Melbourne now for over three years. Her colleagues in the office were very impressed with the level of English she had without ever having lived in an English-speaking country. She admitted that while her written English was pretty strong, she only really started understanding slang after living abroad. Claire never thought about her gaps in casual conversations, as she calls them, since her first job involved fairly formal interactions. Living abroad has certainly helped her achieve full native fluency.

I am a big fan of learning languages. The importance of any particular language may change; there is enough written about predicting linguistic trends of the future, so I won't focus on that. My belief is that the cultural aspects of getting into the locals' heads to understand what drives them, to known how to interact better with them, and, thus, how to open up more opportunities and build more choices for an international career are what justifies all the effort you need to put into becoming at least bilingual. Learning the language is also a great cultural adjustment tool, both to facilitate relocation to a new country and to join a new office. I always thought of America as a true melting pot. There are so many people from all over the world in California, and even more so in Silicon Valley. What has been really fascinating is that after moving to Switzerland and later to London, I discovered that the technology scene in both locations is quite diverse. London is really bustling with multilingual, multiskilled entrepreneurial types. Everything is relative. London's ecosystem is growing rapidly and the city welcomes people from all over the world with skills to add to Tech City. I meet so many people here who started out as linguists, like me, and then moved into a variety of business roles in the technology space.

We No Speak Americano

Yolanda Be Cool and DCUP's catchy tune was blasting from every tiny bar doubled up as a dance club in Palma de Mallorca in the summer of 2010. I had to face the reality of my potential return to the United States after a couple of years in Switzerland where I really enjoyed my work and also having access to all the great places Europe had to offer, from skiing to beach vacations, from ancient castles to quiet country houses, and, most importantly, the access to great wines.

Am I now American or am I feeling European again? What does it mean to be European anyway? This time, it's not Eastern Europe with its angst of a recent painful past, lack of opportunities to make money for some and incredible riches for others, with blurry lines of what's legal and what's not. It's the rest of Europe, accessible from the safety of a Swiss expat package. The tune carried on: "You want to be American. We don't speak American. You want to be American."

The linguistic part of a relocation is quite often underestimated when people move between English-speaking countries. It's one thing is to read a book about the differences between American and British English and totally another to actually live it.

That summer I was making a decision about my potential move to the UK. I always enjoyed visiting London. I worked with quite a few people from the UK when I was based in California, and with my move to Switzerland, I was even more closely connected to the UK. I have mentioned before that I speak every language I know with a foreign accent. My English accent has gotten quite complicated, with influences from living in America for nine years, neutralized by two years in Switzerland, and now slightly upgraded by over three years in the UK. Since I am not a natural linguist and not great musically despite eight years of painful piano lessons, I can never pass for a local anywhere anymore. My preference is to claim global citizenship, belonging everywhere and nowhere at the same time.

Having first moved to Geneva, I made a mental note of those Europeans who speak English with a hint of their native accent that even I can easily distinguish with my lack of a musical ear — they don't blend in. The French, Germans, Italians, and Spaniards: you can pretty easily tell where they are from when they speak English. And those Europeans who speak English as natives more often than not had a British accent. So guess what? Suddenly, in Europe, to a lot of people I sounded like an American! Not even an Eastern European! Talk about confused identity.

The next phase of relocation and linguistic adventure began for me with my move to London after Symantec acquired the VeriSign authentication business. Acquisition integrations are a long process when it comes to merging a $1 billion plus purchase with an existing $6 billion revenue organization. Parts of our business had to be reorganized, but there was still the need to run a global sales operation for Website Security Solutions. This was the job for which I moved to London.

The move felt a lot more natural to me than moving from Ukraine to California or from California to Geneva. I was becoming an expert in relocation through all my experiences and my business and personal travel. I felt like I could now move anywhere and not be surprised by anything or stressed by what went into the move.

One thing that was a little bit unexpected was that my English linguistic explorations were far from over. Okay, I admit, it has always been much easier for me to understand American accents. Have you been on one of those conference calls where you dial in with fifty or more other people and you know there is no way you can identify who is talking? People move through the conversation quickly, don't necessarily introduce themselves when they start. and you feel like you cannot possibly keep track of who is who, why they are there, and why whatever they are saying is relevant to you, your team, or to anything at all. Personally for me, if I didn't know anyone on the call, Americans were much easier to remember and Brits were all blurring together. Now after working in London for over two years, I can certainly tell posh accents from less posh accents and can remember who is who almost instantaneously. Well, I'm again getting to 10,000 hours of practice, coined by Malcolm Gladwell. Amazing how it works!

Besides the accents, I could now totally relate to Claire's slang point. While I have completely embraced American culture, including urban slang, and felt absolutely local in California, it suddenly turned out that not only did I have to relearn very simple things in British English but also to make sure I didn't use them at the wrong time. When you get people laughing at you for saying pants instead of trousers, you really get it. Pants means underwear here, folks, not the bottom part of a suit! I will spare you more embarrassing phrases and circumstances; pick up a book on the differences or just live through it yourself!

My least favorite thing was studying for the theory before taking the driving test here in the UK. I actually had to study and learn a whole bunch of new words, from slip roads to dual carriageways, all confusing me along the way. We really underestimate the level of discomfort that we may experience while relearning the terms for the basics that surround us. The flavor of English is the hardest thing for foreigners to get used to when they are first branching out from their own cultures. When you mix it up with peculiar cultural differences, there is a lot of adjustment to do.

How Many Is Good Enough?

You can see that the topic of languages is one of my favorites. Maybe the reason for that is that language was the first thing I learned about in differentiating myself from others and becoming an expert. In my neighborhood, people spoke Russian. The eastern part of Ukraine historically has been predominantly Russian speaking. Learning a foreign language to the extent of being an expert was not on anyone's priority list when I was growing up, until I got to the school where everyone was focused on English. Then everything changed — it wasn't about uniqueness anymore, it was about the level of expertise. My ambition was always to excel. It didn't really matter in what; I just wanted to do better and to show expertise. The funny thing is I never really thought about the practical application of English until much later when it was time to focus on a career choice.

The question about the number of languages I needed haunted me after I achieved a level of expertise in English that opened multiple career options for me. What I know now is that a choice of a language is fairly random when you are young. Later in life it's harder to focus on learning a foreign language if you don't have strong motivation. Unless you are a natural linguist or just a lifelong learning enthusiast, once a language choice provides you with a clear potential economic advantage, you are most likely going to stop learning and focus your time and money on other things.

I grew up bilingual, Russian and Ukrainian. That's two languages right there. Was that enough? Not at all! English held the biggest potential for gaining an economic advantage. Now we are talking about three languages. Was it enough? Sure, careerwise it was perfectly respectable to stop right there. My level of French has never compared with the first three languages; however, it did help me to feel more like a transplant than an expat in Geneva. After that I periodically tried to learn the basics of various languages, sometimes for the sake of understanding someone's culture better, other times for feeling a little more comfortable on a holiday trip.

The Mandarin studies I attempted both as a way to understand Claire better when we worked closely together and as an intellectual challenge has demonstrated that my motivation to excel must be based on some economic potential. Plainly, can I make more money if I invest that much time in learning a particular language? The basics are fun to brag about to nonlinguists and will earn you some respect from native speakers. You will feel that the door to friendship or business relationships opens a little wider. The most recent example for me was an interview I had with a candidate who studied Mandarin in the UK because he was interested in working in China. He could see that job opportunities there were going to require at least Mandarin, and he was really fascinated with the culture. It's great to be able to identify your interests and shape your plans even when you're in college. If you manage to do that, then the question of how many languages are worth your time learning will be answered pretty easily.

Chapter 5
Cultural Adaptation

When in Rome...

I finally went to Rome after a few years of living in Europe. It was a great long weekend trip, a quick journey to magnificent ruins, great restaurants, and impressive churches. We didn't have to do as the Romans do at all. There is no shame in being a tourist. Through all my international relocations I have realized that even with all my world travel experience, I still enjoy being an unattached visitor, going past the sites, taking pictures, being uninvolved.

Our experiences when visiting foreign destinations form around four distinctly different mindsets: a tourist, a student, an expat, and a transplant. The highest degree of culture shock you experience is when your mindset doesn't match your relocation goals.

A tourist comes to see, capture experiences, and quickly retreat back to his or her home country. If you are relocating for a substantial period of time but have the attitude of a tourist, everything will be exciting and different at the start but will feel like a short-term visit. You may not get a chance to learn what you have come to learn or build any meaningful relationships since you have just a transitory state of mind.

A student arrives to learn and party but also has high expectations about what will happen post graduation. If you arrive on a work assignment, you may find that your growth potential is not quite what you imagined. Partying may not be an option either, since not every job will come with long holidays. A student mentality will get you a lot of learning experiences but not necessarily help prepare you for a smart exit. You may feel that everything is still ahead and fundamental questions about goals, post assignment career planning, and the future may not need to be answered now. At some point you will start getting tired of bouncing around and will want to settle down. With that comes the sad reality that your high expectations have passed and you need to actually do some planning to succeed in your next steps.

An expat is reasonably financially secure or at least has his or her needs met. The expat's work contract may not necessarily be the type I have discussed. However, it's all about mentality. An expat's mentality comes with a well-defined job post, a perception about how much the business is investing in you, and high expectations for future opportunities. The danger quite often is in a lack of planning for the future and the fact that you need to localize to continue moving forward. The business that you started with in a foreign location may not have anything for you in terms of the next step.

Localization suddenly means losing a comfortable status. You weren't planning to stay forever anyway, haven't invested into local networks, or have networked mostly with people who share your country of origin or your type of assignment, so it's time to go back or look at the next opportunity. Culturally you are sort of forgiven for not spending time to localize because your assignment was temporary.

My thought is that a transplant mindset is the most productive one for dealing with your short- and long-term stays abroad. This mindset makes you absorb culture shock, whether it's language, weather, food, or local customs, and gets you to jump in with all your heart. Another way of looking at this type of experience is to think of it as maximizing your potential and your opportunity. Learn the language or pick up local slang, network and create friendships, act as a tour guide for friends and family who want to come over, ask questions, and get over your feeling of not belonging. Allow yourself to blossom in the new soil. Don't fall prey to nostalgia for other places you lived in or for the friends you left behind. Bring your friends and family over to share your new experiences. Your outlook on life will be enriched!

The degree of your culture shock upon arrival depends on many factors and your experiences prior to your relocation. How well have you researched your destination? Do you speak the language? Do you have friends who grew up there? Have any of your family members lived there for extended periods of time? How much have you travelled before your first international relocation? What's your financial situation? How much do you need to socialize with the locals? Are you going to build a new network through the school community or your business colleagues? Are you moving alone or with friends or family?

What's culture shock to me may be just a minor inconvenience to you, or vice versa. The shock factor is not the same for everyone. Some people think of their experiences abroad as lacking comfort or feeling awkwardness. Many of these feelings are different manifestations of culture shock, feeling disconnected from your expectations and from reality. The women in this book were prepared for their moves to various degrees. One thing that stands out for me is that all of them had more of a transplant mentality: they had somewhat of a fighter's attitude with a high degree of tolerance for change. They also were very independent, mostly because of their upbringing and the experiences they had prior to their first move abroad. Sure, they had some fears and doubts about whether the move would be a success but, at the core, they didn't rely on anyone to make their international relocations possible.

Back in Seattle, at a coffee shop, I was trying to get to the core of what formed Karen's independence. She was shy growing up. The change came after being sent to summer camps in Colorado. Girls had to learn first aid, horseback riding, and mountain climbing. Most importantly, the trips were about gaining experience with new people away from her family and forming good social habits like learning how to be competitive without being hostile.

Karen is a very confident, independent, and career-focused woman. Having travelled to five continents, she enjoys being taken out of her element, which is exactly what her relocations did for her. They exposed her to new experiences. She says she was always so excited and open to change: it awakens senses. Culture shock wasn't really something she ever felt. Having grown up in the United States, Karen was always interested in the international community, news, and information in general. She was probably more prepared than a lot of people since she always tried to learn about countries she wanted to experience and researched them prior to relocation. Karen was usually aware of changes she was going to encounter so she was able to successfully adapt before she arrived.

We talked about the rewards of international relocation. For Karen they are making new friends for a lifetime and understanding the world in a different way. When you transplant, you have to adapt and your social environment and natural curiosity are strong environmental success factors. Being prepared and having an open mind for things ahead enhances your ability to adjust and will substantially reduce culture shock.

The more different your destination of origin from your destination of choice, the more you will face the likelihood of experiencing culture shock and having difficulties with adaptation. Try transplanting palm trees to Stockholm.... Karen's first international move was to South Africa. Having moved twice in the United States, she settled in California. Okay, maybe climatewise, this was actually not such a far-off move. If you are relocating from California to start experiencing the weather in Britain, the wonder about how bad British weather is actually will be a source of many conversations you will have.

I wondered if Karen moving from one of the strongest economies in the world to a country with a painful recent past, big disparities in incomes, and high crime rates would provide a good example of culture shock for my book. To my surprise, Karen felt confident, prepared, and excited about relocating to South Africa for a short-term assignment. She made great friendships, saw the country, enjoyed her work, and had good social experiences. This story reinforces the importance of preparation, understanding what you are likely to encounter and jumping in without fear.

Having experience in previously moving as a child or adult has a major impact on your adaptability. So does the experience of being on your own and being thrown into social situations. It boosts your self-awareness and confidence. Karen has moved and observed her family moves. She was aware of her needs and the world around her. She could still could be surprised, maybe not shocked, but at the same time the moves didn't cause her too much stress and inconvenience.

Let's go back to Ekaterina's story, one of the four Russian MBA students I met at San Jose State University. I wanted to explore whether moving for economic advantage was likely to increase the shock factor. Do we all suffer from a "poor relative syndrome" or was it just my attitude during my first move from Ukraine to California? I remember feeling lost in California, not understanding where people were coming from in social situations, having no idea about cultural references to films and TV shows or even music. The worst part was my self-image: worrying about not being able to afford anything and feeling awkward about the quality and style of my clothes. Let's be frank: young Ukrainian women were not particularly known for their classy dress code during the late 1990s. I wasn't the exception.

Ekaterina comes from a military service family. Her father was the one in the service. The family moved with him. Many times! Most of the moves were local, within the same region in Russia, but there were also longer relocations to the completely different world of Russia's Far East. Ekaterina also experienced life abroad, a very rare opportunity for inhabitants of the Soviet Union. Her family moved to Germany. The military base was in the forest. People there socialized in Russian and were really isolated from the lives and experiences of locals. Ekaterina herself is not sure whether these moves prepared her for her first big move to California.

She views moving as a child as too passive, with parents settling all matters. There was nothing for her to worry about apart from losing friends and having to make new ones with every move.

My theory is that moving as a child builds up your resilience. All these events of losing friends, living in new towns, and having new experiences add up. You begin to expect the unexpected. I agree with Ekaterina that the new level of responsibility is a challenge but culturally you become more adjusted to the transient nature of your lifestyle.

She gave me a few new items in the "I found this odd" category. They certainly are not shocking but quite funny as to how our perceptions of situations and people were completely aligned. The firemen story is my favorite. This was before we all saw that one episode of "Sex and the City" about firemen. One of her American acquaintances, a woman in her thirties, was insisting that Ekaterina and her friends must meet the firemen in San Jose. I can just see it in the form of a comic strip, with a cute blond girl with gorgeous long hair rolling her eyes and the text bubble over her head saying, "They are fat, ugly, and drunk. Why do we need to see them?" Indeed, if you grew up in Russia in the 1980s, that would be your perception of people at the fire station. Hotness and firemen didn't go together at that time in Russian or Ukrainian cities.

Empty streets in California were another oddity. If you live in the middle of Silicon Valley outside of San Francisco and are not in one of the miniature downtowns, you don't see a lot of people walking around. Everyone drives. Everything is built and planned for car owners. There is a huge number of drivethroughs. Even Starbucks is a drivethrough. Public transportation is not developed at all. We all found this odd mostly because in our first year of living in California, none of us could afford a car. It was quite awkward to constantly beg friends with cars for rides. Public transportation connections as an alternative added extreme amounts of time to the daily commute. I am willing to add transportation problems to my list of culturally shocking things! It certainly takes a lot of adaptation and planning: bus connections, train connections, and, of course, walking shoes.

Interviewing Julia on Skype, I discovered that her feelings about moving from Ryazan to California were quite different from Ekaterina's. She admitted that before moving she was somewhat of a spoiled brat. The move away from her family helped her quickly grow up and become responsible for herself. I asked all my interview subjects about their top three most difficult things about their relocations. For Julia, they were switching from spoken tests, common in Russian education, to written tests typical in the U.S. system, learning slang, and her sudden freedom, meaning her getting away from her fairly strict parents. None of these was particularly related to culture shock. I kept digging and asked her for more stories about her first days in California.

There it was: another line added to the complex pattern of having to be in the know and yet not knowing. One of Julia's vivid memories is getting lost inside one of Macy's department stores. For me, Macy's was a place where I had to take a job that required little training and helped me earn a few extra dollars one Christmas season to pay the bills. For Julia Macy's was a place of frustration and unfamiliar surroundings. She ended up in front of a mirrored wall, crying, and not knowing how to find the exit. It may seem silly today but just fifteen years earlier, there was nothing like Macy's where Julia grew up. It was probably the peak of her frustration with many associated odd, unfamiliar, and incomprehensible things about it such as a fear of asking too many questions and a general unsettled feeling that nothing around her fit. Having Google maps on an iPhone seems like an easy solution to Julia's problem today, but then it was not so simple.

Fifteen years ago the problem was one of getting lost. Today, newly relocated people from Russia are likely going to find other things frustrating. Julia's underlying issue was leaving her comfort zone and not having a quick fix for any problem that arose. Life with her parents was familiar; no demonstration of her independence was required until she packed her suitcases and moved to the United States. Julia's parents, their parents, and great-grandparents all lived in the same city. Three generations had their roots in the same place. When she was a child, the family didn't travel much. Julia recalls a total of perhaps six trips altogether, with St. Petersburg being the farthest destination. She was not very well prepared for America's abundance of choices and the grandeur of shopping mall architecture. She tells this Macy's maze story as a curious anecdote to address one minor culturally shocking or rather surprising issue. Her tale is full of humor and the realization of how much experience we lacked. This is what she moved to the United States for, gaining experience and satisfying her curiosity about the world. It was a lucky coincidence that the sponsors who she worked with were from Northern California. Other parts of the United States, as she later discovered, might not have offered the same life-changing opportunity.

Julia is very confident about herself, her abilities, her relationship-building skills, and most of all, about where she belongs. She calls herself a true Californian. Colorado was a surprising and bold move for her, without much research or preparation, so that she could experience something completely different from California. It was an experiment in lifestyle. Julia's key point is that only when you move away from "your kind of place" do you find out what you are missing. California, or to be more precise, Silicon Valley was truly a melting pot. It had been like that for dozens of years. Being from somewhere else is really what being a true Californian is about, adding your experience into the mix. An incident with a xenophobic lawyer in Colorado wasn't what prompted Julia's move back to California. It was a realization of what she really appreciated: the openness of life in the Valley, the abundance of professional choices, the great weather, and the people from all over the world. She is also able to apply her MBA degree in California in ways that make her quite an unusual sales person for her industry. She is focused on complex international deals, global contracts, and elegant solutions to business operations. To be frank, even in culturally homogeneous Colorado, Julia found that her international background had an edge. Most people liked that she was different. Some of the jobs she held she had gotten because she was different and had broader experience than other candidates. The Colorado business environment in the end didn't provide her with what she required for a great work experience (fun, freedom, and money) in the same way that California did.

Julia mentioned something that struck a chord with me as one of the most difficult parts of her relocation, even though it was further down on the list: money matters. Moving to attain an economic advantage can be incredibly rewarding for the future and a huge boost to self-esteem, but also can cause a lot of pain in the early days of relocation. Now that we have seen financial crises rippling through the world during our lifetimes, it's clear that the way nations handle money is correlated fairly strongly with how individuals handle money within those countries. Michael Lewis' great book, *Boomerang*, explores this phenomenon in depth. You keep doing things you know when you live within a certain economy. For our transplant stories, money-handling habits add a new angle to the cultural adjustment journey. I personally felt poor in Ukraine, irrational in the United States, secure in Switzerland, and taken advantage of in the UK. These feelings also coincided with how my financial situation had been evolving and the type of income I was able to generate at different stages of my career. It's quite interesting how my income reflected the realities of the respective nations and their knowledge workers.

Julia's thoughts about irrationality in the United States have to do with the availability of "magic cards." We former Soviets came from a cash-based society. If you didn't have money for something urgent, you went to your friends and family to borrow it. There was no interest and no contract, just a word of honor. Sometimes that word was broken. Most of the time you got your money back and built a web of favors.

We got to the United States and ran into an amazingly bizarre ease of accessing pretty hefty credit lines. Julia put it best: "We were poor and then we discovered magic cards. It took years to pay them off!" It was one of those perfectly sunny days in California; school had just started, and we were strolling through the campus of San Jose State University. There was sun, palm trees, international student crowds, tables near the cafeteria showcasing various university services, and a stand from a major credit card company. The temptation was right there. We all had a support system to sustain us at the poverty line, as defined by the minimum income standard of California, be it a scholarship from school or from a friendly local church. We had confidence that if we just got through these couple of short years, the jobs will be there and the debts will quickly get erased. We couldn't get loans from banks without someone acting as a co-guarantor, so credit cards provided the fix for us, but also introduced us to a massive financial burden. It took an amazing amount of discipline and a number of personal finance self-help books to pay them off.

As an expat or, even better, as a lucky soul on an intercompany transfer arrangement, you will be more secure in your revenue-generating ability. There is no comparison to poor Eastern European students! What may be somewhat of a shock is how much energy you will likely need to invest in reconciling taxes across multiple geographies. Doing research in tax reconciliation, finding the right advisors locally, getting a good idea of fiscal and calendar year differences between countries, and understanding your company's policies on what is offered as part of your package are very good ways of reducing your level of surprise in the first tax year. Otherwise, the shock is likely to be beyond just a cultural one.

Olga and I were sitting on the beach in Odessa, the pearl of the Black Sea as the old Russian pop song puts it, reminiscing about our school and our past work. I asked her about some examples of culture shock in her days in California. She was not an exception to the money matters surprises and reminded me of a completely different aspect about this. Americans have gotten so dependent on plastic (debit or credit cards) that people don't really carry cash to the malls anymore. Olga stunned a cashier at a Nordstrom's cash register by presenting a crisp $100 bill at some point. Our views change so quickly as we adapt to our new environments. I can't imagine walking into a mall with a bunch of cash any longer but Olga reminded me that it's normal for people to bring cash while shopping even for substantial purchases in Russia. At the same time, the first ABBA museum in Stockholm (my tourist example) did not accept cash at all but for a noble reason: to eliminate crime since many illegal dealings are transacted in cash.

There are many areas of our daily lives that will need to be adjusted, from figuring out how to find a doctor to placing your children into a school that best fits them. The women I interviewed didn't necessarily identify their top difficulties on the adaptability list with culture shock. Perhaps I am being overly dramatic in emphasizing culture shock. Let's explore further.

Olga listed infrastructure as her most difficult thing that impacts the ease of relocation abroad. The following items are not on our mind when we move but they certainly overcomplicate our lives when we are undergoing a relocation: finding an apartment, figuring out how to pay for gas and electricity, determining what a country charges in taxes and for what items, buying a mobile phone, and connecting a land line. All these items Olga found most annoying to deal with. I would add that in some countries, they really are shocking. My most surprising discovery with my move to the UK was that the bureaucracy in a few areas rivals that of the Soviet Union in the early 1980s. Dealing with "infrastructure" is truly painful. It takes a few weeks to get Internet and phone equipment shipped, the choices are limited, prices are high, and the quality is doubtful. When you finally manage to set up your Internet connection, it is so slow that watching a movie on Netflix and trying to access anything else at the same time shuts your wireless router down. Now compare this with the high-speed Internet connection that my mom and dad boast in their modest Ukrainian apartment. It's night and day! I am not sure which of these options is more culturally shocking to me. Most likely, as young Ukrainians grow up they will feel exactly like I do about the UK's Internet access, having experienced blazing speeds in California offices early on.

Some of my examples were meant to show the nuisance that they were. However, culture shock can be a huge impediment to adjusting to your new home country. The surprise factor is not as important as how well you will handle things that are outside your comfort zone. Your reactions will help ensure that you enjoy your environment and focus on the positives of your experience. Bureaucracy can be managed if you have the right attitude. Most successful people with international careers adapt well, figure things out, or find support networks that will help them identify the differences and learn to manage them. Doing research and managing expectations will contribute to your success when replanting yourself and your family into a new environment.

Reverse Culture Shock

I always thought that reverse culture shock was a myth. How can someone possibly forget where they grew up and how things were? The more people I talk to, the more I realize that it's a very real phenomenon. We move on and grow out of our old habits, living conditions, the way our immediate surroundings were, and the aspirations that we had at one time and one place. Quite often, when you return to a community that doesn't change very much, many things surprise you, even within the same country. Other times, life in our homeland changes so dramatically that we lose touch completely.

My first trip back to Ukraine was two years after I had left. It was uncomfortable. I got used to higher standards of customer service, nonsmoking restaurants and hotels, better roads, well-lit streets, and the permanent availability of hot and cold water from the tap. All of these things were minor but made a huge difference and created my new comfort zone. There was a mix of nostalgia and surprise in my perception of what the living conditions and attitudes were when I returned to Ukraine.

If you disconnect from your old reality completely, it is quite difficult to dive right back in. It's even more true if you don't stay in touch with a lot of people with whom you grew up. Reverse culture shock to me is not so much about physical things or the environment but about how behaviors and attitudes in the place you left behind have not changed or, even more to the point, how they have evolved in a different unexpected direction, without your knowledge. Pop culture, movie references, news coverage, all of these things continue evolving in their very localized direction but you have taken a different turn. I have met people, however, who manage to preserve their cultural ethos completely in their new environment and keep up to date on the changes and developments in their country of origin.

The flip side is that our time to consume information is limited. If we choose not to immerse ourselves in our new local culture, to keep friends from our motherland, and try really hard not to blend in with the locals, surely when we return home, we experience no major shock to our system. Things are as expected. What we miss out on is really understanding the new place where we have lived.

Julia hadn't been back to Russia in a long time. She arranged to meet her mother and a friend in Kiev. This was the first visit to Ukraine for her American husband. In talking to her mother and her friend, Julia had more of a reverse culture shock than her husband had in being in Ukraine. Ukraine and Russia were not really miles apart culturally.

Ukrainian life was a bit calmer, aspirations were a little less grand, and Wild West capitalism was less wild in Ukraine.

Julia confessed she didn't know how she was going to feel. When she got there, she loved the city and the people. She was nervous and uncomfortable on the way there and not sure what to expect. She enjoyed the trip, the food, the parks, and realized that being the foreigner could be an advantage — the locals do want to make a foreign tourist's experience a happy one.

When I first went back home I remember thinking I now understood why foreigners were taking pictures of bathrooms back in the days when we worked as interpreters in Russia and Ukraine in the 1990s. The standard of living and general conditions in a lot of emerging economies really vary. You meet a lot of people with great education and a great deal of knowledge in many areas of business, politics, and culture, yet you encounter horrible infrastructure problems everywhere. The state of the roads is still awful and so are the drivers, or rather driving etiquette and law enforcement. Then again, have you tried driving in Italy?

To me reverse culture shock has a lot to do with the loss of our original identity and the fear of reverting back. We may not like who we once were. Depending on how deeply we integrated, it can be really painful to replant back. Even temporary visits cause discomfort if you are from a country where the infrastructure needs revamping badly and your new country is pretty advanced. You start taking things for granted, as you should. The higher your ability to focus on the emotion and the positives of relocation and travel in general, the less likely you are going to be shocked. Then again, circumstances vary.

It was a cold winter, a typical winter that foreigners imagine Ukrainian winters to be. I was attempting to fly out from a small local airport in the eastern part of the country which boasted several international flights a day. The plane broke down, the airport had very little heating, the delay was twelve hours, and crowds of people were getting angrier. Every person who had a ticket had to be rebooked on a new flight. The delay turned into a cancellation. This happens anywhere in the world, right? It's the rudeness of the crowd that was really getting to me: people pushing and shoving at the window, just like in the good old 1980s when I was growing up and watched people lined up for hours to buy sausage, cheese, or whatever other culinary delights were made available on that day by the central distribution system. Now, the scene at the airport was only eleven years ago. I was still new to being a transplant but my reverse culture shock seemed to have peaked. Appalling service. How dare they! Where is security when you need it?

Fast forward and I am at the main international airport in Kiev 11 years later. The transfer between the terminals was still a bit awkward but the people were nice, service was much better, and free WiFi was available throughout the airport. The UK's popular chain, Costa Coffee, had opened up its first location in Ukraine. The general feeling of a positive travel experience was there. Despite the fact that you still had to walk outside between terminals without a real transfer, literally starting your check-in process all over again if you were making a domestic travel connection, the food was not of a really high quality, and the cab drivers outside were a bit too pushy, I was not phased by anything that was going on around me. Have I gained more confidence as a traveller or was it the general improvement in the fundamentals of running a country and an airport? The truth is, it was a little bit of both.

Sandra and I met through her husband, Jean-Marc, my former colleague from my days of working in Switzerland, and a transplant himself. Born and raised in France, years ago he moved to England to play music, with no strong English language skills to speak of, and now he was a very successful software salesman. I shared the concept for this book with both of them and Sandra had volunteered to contribute to my research. She was a perfect candidate to further shape my story, having been born in Spain and now become a Londoner.

Sandra had her sights set on London since her early school days. Growing up in Barcelona gave her an immediate exposure to two different cultures from the start. She believes there is now a lot stronger presence of Catalan in schools than when she studied. English was always a big interest for her, and with her sister relocating to London to pursue a better salary package and lifestyle, it became a no brainer for her to go to London, too. It was pretty difficult for her to blend in as the language barrier turned out to be higher than she expected. I have heard this from other multilingual people who didn't travel much before their first move abroad, and I experienced it myself. There is an enormous gap between an ability to read and understand a language and a level of language comfort to start socializing every day. Luckily, Sandra is quite talented in terms of her ability to learn new languages, so she persevered and succeeded.

This part of the story is about her return. Several years later, Sandra was enjoying her life in the UK but needed to get a certain type of job to get into the space that she was always fascinated with: consumer brands. Shoe or clothing manufacturers, it didn't really matter, as long as the brand had a soul and appealed to her. Having worked in the service industry in London to get started, she realized that to break into a type of brand she would be excited about, she had to return to Barcelona and eventually work her way back.

We sat down at a coffee shop near one of the tube stations north of London to talk about Sandra's return to Spain. I really wanted to know about her reverse culture shock and whether the return home was a happy experience. What made her comeback interesting was that Sandra always viewed it as an interim solution. This return was just a stepping stone for launching into a career with an interesting brand. She joined Now, a brand in Barcelona focused on outdoorsy and adventurous lifestyles. Having lived away for five years, Sandra didn't feel any shock or discomfort. Her family support network was there, so the relocation back wasn't too brutal of an experience. One thing that this stint back home did for her was to reinforce why she left in the first place. Growing up, she always wanted to be on the move, go somewhere, and see something new. She was not in a position to travel a lot before she left for London but if there was ever an opportunity to get on a train and get out of town, to gain new experiences, Sandra was always up for it. A lot of people she was friends with preferred to stay where they knew everything. When she returned, things had not changed much for a lot of people. On the one hand, this made it easier for her to reconnect with friends and family; on the other hand, it highlighted that the times could stand still. And that was precisely what she didn't want to experience. This observation wasn't really a big shock for her but more like one of the things to be expected from the place where she grew up.

Reverse culture shock depends on how long you have been away and how much the place and the people who you grew up with have changed. Changes could be good and bad. The experiences I have observed and discussed are not extreme. We are not talking about a return to countries that have suddenly become war zones while we were away. Our observations are about our own adaptability skills, our management of our expectations, and our skills at facing the known and the unknown. One thing that we should bear in mind is the old adage that it's always easier for those who leave than for those who stay to manage expectations. What doesn't work is to return as a complainer and keep telling everyone you know how shockingly bad things are and how you cannot possibly believe that you are the only one who has made any progress.

One System — Multiple Shocks

So you have moved once, twice, maybe even three times. Does it actually get easier? Or do you always feel like it's a huge hill to climb every time? Practice works even with international relocations. I must admit that my comfort level had gone tremendously up after the second time. The past seven years have been pretty interesting in terms of business and personal travel and, of course, relocations. I am used to having mildly amusing interactions at various passport control offices. The latest one was with a young border patrol guard in the UK who looked at my passport, looked at me, and said, "Wow, well travelled!" I felt something of a feeling of pride. Generally border patrol guards are not that easily impressed. This must mean I'm reaching the stage when people around me assume that I'm very worldly and can take on any kind of travel-related challenge, relocation or not.

It's not just about taking on another move. It's also about managing your own expectations and changing circumstances. If we all were at one and the same reasonably high level of financial security, lots of headaches would simply go away. What continues to cause shocks to the systems of even very well-travelled experienced people is how to do a lot with limited resources in terms of money, time, and opportunity.

Returning to the move to Switzerland, it was the second international move for Karen as well as for me. We shouldn't even be talking about the shock factor in this case, right? Switzerland is the symbol of neutrality and politeness. How hard can it be? If you move past the language barrier in social situations, it really is the most convenient country in the world in many respects. Having moved from California to Switzerland, I felt well-adjusted right away. The fact that I knew Karen and other people in the office helped create an instantaneous social network.

I agree with Olga's assessment: infrastructure is really one of the most shocking adjustments we have to make when moving abroad. Everything is perfect in Switzerland. Trains run on time, people don't rush, and everything works. However, the world stops spinning on Sundays. Everything is closed. For those of us who relocate because we work and go for international assignments, it's highly likely that we spend quite an extraordinary amount of hours in the office, have to stay pretty late to accommodate our U.S. colleagues, and generally don't have a life like most normal Swiss citizens do. Running errands, shopping, arranging for any kind of work done at the place you are renting are certainly at the top of my list of shockingly inconvenient things.

I probably get adjusted to new living conditions too much and too quickly. Having gone completely native in California, as a result I was used to 24-hour, seven-day-a-week megastores that sold pretty much anything and shopping malls that were open late into the night. Services, beauty or medical, were the easiest thing to arrange and practically no wait was required. Moving to Switzerland, compared to my first experience of going from Ukraine to California, was going to be a breeze. I almost fell into the trap that many Americans fall into: the world must work the same way everywhere, at least in the "developed" economies it does, right? To be fair, nothing was extremely shocking in Switzerland. I probably surprised myself by having very firm expectations that everything was going to be at my fingertips. This was more a problem of arrogance in having some experience and a point of comparison.

My surprises and shocks in Northern California were primarily grounded in a complete lack of experience with lifestyles outside of the former Soviet Union. The abundance of everything, the ease of getting credit cards, the ability to get houses and cars on credit that no one is really able to afford, huge gaps between the money made by talented tech entrepreneurs and engineers and everyone else, all of that was a brand new reality that I was able to experience right before the dot-com bust. All this experience came before my full understanding of what dot-com, boom or bust, really meant.

While the language barrier was not really a huge issue in Geneva, I did have my regrets about never taking French to the level of fluency at the university. Women all over the world would agree that while we may laugh off the issue of not being able to talk to our hairdresser, it does get a bit frustrating. It's one of those minor annoyances that spoil all the fun of the experience. I was going to one of the fashionable salons close to Rue du Rhône, the main shopping drag in Geneva, and tried really hard to explain myself to an Italian hairdresser who didn't speak any English but had made some progress in conversational French. Since this was the time before Tabletop Translator kinds of apps, I had to muddle my way through without any funny exchanges and missed out on the usual salon banter.

Then there are, of course, medical services. Generally, I don't need to visit doctors to reassure myself that I'm healthy. However, things do go wrong sometimes, particularly when you start learning how to ski at a pretty advanced age because you want to maximize the advantages of living in Switzerland. This is where I admitted my defeat and looked up names of medical professionals who spoke English or at least Russian. The idea of trying to explain any anatomy-related issues in French was simply overwhelming. Also, the whole process of searching for doctors and booking appointments in a short window of business hours during the week only was quite a shock. With that also comes another infrastructure-related point: don't go anywhere without being clear on who will be paying your medical expenses. I know we all complain about how expensive the American health care system is, how not everyone is covered, and so on. Try other countries! The Swiss system was great but very expensive, so the need for the proper set-up of insurance and understanding of how to use it was really important. The UK is great in that respect, since the services are free. However, you may have to wait for a really long time to address your particular problem. Having private insurance from your employer in the UK does help.

One of my Swiss friends, Christina, validated my view about service appointments. Whenever I needed anything fixed in my Geneva flat, the availability of appointment was limited to short business hours only. Christina mentioned that she found this appalling, too. It's almost as if women are still expected to be at home to look after the things that need arranging and fixing. I couldn't pick up subtlety in stumbling through my requests in French. However, more than once I heard that Madame was expected to sit and wait for an undefined or poorly defined number of hours until a particular service agent finally completed his rounds and made his way to her dwelling. Get an apartment with a concierge service is my advice, and prepare to explain yourself in French. I did resort to translation assistance from my multilingual Swiss colleagues when I was at the verge of desperation.

One big positive infrastructure-related point and a good kind of shock was that at that time in Switzerland you could get out of your annual phone contract. Having dealt with American phone and Internet providers, I was expecting to have to pay up when breaking the contract early. However, in Switzerland it was as simple as writing a letter explaining that my employment contract had ended and I was relocating to another country because our business had been acquired. It was a small thing but it really made me happy — the mobile contract was quite expensive.

None of these things is a huge barrier against making a life in a foreign country a great success. Asking for advice and understanding how the peculiarities of everyday life work in your fluent or semifluent language can help you get adjusted very quickly. We also have somewhat of internal adjustment clock. My belief is that naturally some people will always adjust much faster than most of us. I need about six months before the novelty starts wearing off and the place and the circumstances become really familiar. What's interesting is that I never expected I would literally feel at home in multiple countries. I now do. That feeling of coming home in today's world of travel and relocation is not really about where you were born and lived with your parents, but about where you spend significant periods of your time. It actually makes me just a little nostalgic to fly into one of the familiar airports, go through the places I know well, and, most of all, seeing people who I met and became friends with there.

All of that said, Switzerland was the place that made me most happy being there. I did agree with the assessment of Switzerland in Eric Weiner's book investigating countries by their degree of happiness. Generally, interactions with people make me happy. I have the luxury of constantly learning and enjoying interactions with people in any country of the world where I live or just travel to. Switzerland for me will always be a special and happy place. I loved the pace, the nature, and its proximity to other exciting destinations in Europe as well as its amazing, quite avant-garde opera performances at the Grand Opera de Genève.

One more thing to throw into our culture shock discussion is transportation. Transportation was a big change to manage throughout all of my moves. The amount of time we spend getting to and from places of work, fun, and travel destinations is really shocking. Many of us saw adjustments both in terms of experience and perception of what owning a car means in different countries and whether a car is just a matter of convenience or also a status symbol.

In Ukraine, owning a car was a sign of financial success. It's still the same today. Not everyone can afford one. One car per family is far from a reality even today but the taxi services have gotten much better. I was driving an old beat-up Ford and was very proud of joining the ranks of driving-induced affluence. Moving to California without being able to afford a car presented a real issue.

While my Russian friends were talking about streets being empty as somewhat of a culture shock, I was more depressed about the fact that I had abandoned the convenience of a fifteen-minute drive to work for a two-hour journey each way by bus, train, and shuttle to school. It wasn't really an abandonment of that convenience as much as an investment in my American dream, which I fully believe I have gotten a high return on. The truth was that it took me a while to get to the point of that fifteen-minute drive to work. I started out at having a two-and-a-half-hour morning commute to work, then a fifteen-minute commute to school, and then a two-hour return commute in the evening. This was at the beginning of my first career teaching in Ukraine. Being able to finally have a short drive to work, being independent, and keeping away from crowds felt amazing. Sure, taking a taxi would have been much cheaper but the whole status thing did contribute to a decision to own even a low-quality old car.

My culture shock in California was rooted in a complete change of status: losing eloquence, since knowing the language and understanding the realities of the local lifestyle were two very different things; going from teaching at a university to being taught and having to be graded again; having even less disposable income and amassing credit card debt; and, on top of all that, being lucky to rent a room in a beautiful house in the middle of one of the richest cities in Silicon Valley but having to cope with an extreme commute to San Jose State University. My first big purchase, as soon as I could afford it, was, of course, a car. A little more than a year later it died quietly on a turn onto a highway; luckily, its death did not cause a major accident. By then I could afford a better car and got an almost new, speedy convertible Miata. I was on top of the world! At the same time jobs and apartments had changed so I got back to that dream of a fifteen-minute drive if the traffic was fine, with my convertible top down so that I could enjoy beautiful spring and summer days that lasted most of the year.

Fast-forward to the move to Switzerland. In 2008 I consciously chose not to bother to own a car again. Because I could! Everything works in Switzerland as far as transport is concerned. Geneva is a fairly small city, and living in an apartment somewhat in the central part of the city offered a fantastic opportunity to walk everywhere on the weekends. I also had a fairly quick, forty-minute commute to work. Part of this decision was the feeling of having only a short-term stay in Switzerland, which was a bit of an expat mentality. In retrospective, I wouldn't have bought a car even if I stayed longer. Switzerland is a great country to travel in by train. Going skiing, sightseeing, or visiting friends can all be done by train or a combination of train and other types of public transportation. It's a fairly expensive way to travel, depending on your location and your interests. You could run up a few thousand francs in transportation expenses a year, but it still feels less wasteful than dealing with driving, maintaining, and parking your car if you are a city dweller. I love cities, not suburbs, so being able to have a little apartment close to a bus stop actually made a huge contribution to my overall happiness.

My examples are about tackling new living conditions on your own. Moving with dependents or with equals throws in additional challenges or makes it easier.

Olga's move to Odessa had simplified her life, an experience not dissimilar to mine. She was used to driving in California, and then braved driving in Moscow's city center. When she finally moved to Odessa, there was really no point to buying a car. Living in the city center and not having to commute to a remote or generally inaccessible part of the city made the choice simple. My choice in London was the same. I live in one of the towns in Greater London, and for a year I commuted to London's fashionable (among tech startups) Bricklane, north of the City of London, every day. Dealing with driving and parking would only have caused me unnecessary stress and reduced my opportunities to read or reply to various emails or check out the most recent social media gossip. When I travel back to California and talk to the same group of friends about cars, those who live in San Francisco understand, but those who are in the middle of Silicon Valley can't imagine their lives without cars.

One of the most exciting things for those of us who transplant well is to have an opportunity to compare living conditions, habits, cultures, and our experiences of growing roots in various dream destinations. I have found it easier to move up in comfort and convenience every time. Even if I judge by the happiness index of the overall population of the country alone, going from Ukraine to the United States and then to Switzerland is the road up in comfort and convenience. The UK is not bad, too. Those who live here know that by not bad, we actually mean great. There are things besides the happiness index that I personally adore about London, like its architecture and theater, things that make me disregard the minor inconveniences of everyday life which I wouldn't have in Switzerland or the United States. The climb up in experience is relative. In talking to people who made lateral moves or moves down in comfort from country to country, they were well prepared for the surprises and minor shocks awaiting them. We can all adjust. It's important to actually want to do it. It does get easier after a few tries. We draw upon our experience and feel empowered by our knowledge. After all, culture and new life experience count for a lot more than a high-speed Internet connection.

Chapter 6
Career Changes

Moving Out to Move Up

My most important career lesson so far has been that you always should tell people who work with you what your interests and aspirations are. Don't be shy about sharing how mobile, flexible, and interested in working internationally you are, particularly if you are not yet in the executive ranks. You do need to work harder to be heard. To us it may feel awkward and too far reaching at times, but not to the people we talk to. The timing has to be right but we all go to enough work parties, lunches, and after-work get togethers to have opportunities for informal discussions about our lives and aspirations.

I will refrain from focusing on career advice for women versus men. In my personal experience, the basics of interactions regarding seeking advice and sharing knowledge have been the same for both women and men. Having met enough shy men who needed advice, men who wanted to advance by looking for mentors or sponsors, and men who were very determined, and have met go-getter type women who pushed past a lot of challenges, I have seen a more equally balanced approach to opportunities than statistics show us. As managers, we need to look at the core of our employees' career and relocation interests and skills and hear what excites them, what drives them.

What has been true is that a lot more women approached me and wanted to share and talk about what they were doing or what they would like to do than men did. I don't like generalizing whether men or women are more likely to seek advice, particularly regarding international moves, because a lot of these conversations are so situational. One thing I will admit to is that having moved abroad three times, I have met a lot of women in various business and social settings who have done the same thing. We end up eagerly swapping our wanderer stories. And sometimes we swap them more eagerly when we meet people who share our native language.

In early 2013, I was returning to London from visiting Olga in Odessa. I ended up sitting next to a young woman, Svetlana, who was travelling with her daughter. Svetlana looked over my shoulder as I was typing on my slightly dated and, thus, less glamorous Macbook Pro and asked me whether I was writing a book. As a first-time author to be, I was really flattered and had a fun half hour sharing the concept of this book and why I thought it was important to encourage other women who are just beginning their international journey.

My neighbor was really interested in the idea and happened to be a transplant herself. She had studied in Turkey, felt very comfortable and adjusted there, returned to Ukraine with a plan to try another location, and now was on her way to live in Switzerland for some time. She was another naturally curious person, and I had a great discussion about what she would have loved to have learned before her first move. My point is that we learn about international opportunities everywhere: having coffee with a colleague in the office, flying to a holiday destination, and meeting for dinner after an all-day team event with new people.

The ability to share and ask questions will take you one step closer to your dreams of new and exciting destinations. Sometimes people will volunteer to help, while at other times you will have to push for help and justify your intent. Having clarity about your objectives and skill in sharing them without pressure but in a way that engages people, will help you find others who will match you to the opportunities they come across. "Ah, that woman from the London office who I met at a really nice dinner we had with the EMEA team. She said she would love to work in the UK. If there were a sales position coming up in London, she would move right away, not a problem. Oh, and she has worked internationally from the California office for several years now." Things actually do work that way. If you are memorable, your objectives are clear, and you engage with people well, it will help with an international move as well as with anything else you are doing in your career.

So you have resolved to find ways to move abroad but don't have enough money to just go and try it out without a job. The good news is that many companies, small and large, are looking for talented people who are mobile. I don't need to spend a lot of time explaining just how much more convenient it is to land opportunities within the same enterprise. It's significantly easier to find people to talk to who can help at the right time, but this doesn't mean that you don't need to work at it. As with anything in your career and in life, a dose of luck helps, but internal networking still requires effort and strong navigation skills.

There are some locations where it's a lot more natural and not even that difficult to plan and execute your life and career move. There are others where it may appear like an impossible dream. The worse your country's economy, the more impossible it looks. Think of the days when the Soviet Union collapsed. It all comes down to formulating your plan and following through. My experience as well as the experiences of most of the women I spoke with was in high tech, with a couple of exceptions. There are many possibilities for those of us in the technology industry to keep on moving around the globe. Education, language skills, and having previous experience as part of an international team are all factors that increase your chances of a successful outcome to claim your first relocation abroad.

It is encouraging to know that the larger the company is, the more of a chance you have to stumble upon a whole department that is focused on relocation and that will be there to assist you. If you have never attempted a move abroad, you may not even realize how common relocation is for most midsize to large companies. Small businesses happily relocate their employees as well and help them with visas at the destination if they are recruiting them out from another contract. Timing, particular skill, your price tag: all of these elements become important in having an international relocation or localization contract drafted for you. Getting there is about searching, making your intentions known, and never closing the door to a discussion. You may or may not jump into your first move abroad on your first try, but practice is good for international relocation interviews. Not every opportunity is going to be the right one. The destination may be perfect but the job may not be a great fit. The job may be amazing but the destination may not be your dream or may even pose some dangers and may be far from your lifestyle expectations. You have to look at the whole package when you make a choice.

What I mean by moving out to move up is that quite often opportunities for advancement of your career, your learning, and your experience are somewhere abroad within the company for which you currently work. Identifying them and having informal conversations with people who can help sponsor you are really important. What's even more important is to be able to create a job for yourself in the location that you have your eyes set on. People with job and opportunity creation skills also create value for the business they are in. If you are able to clearly articulate what value you are going to bring, many managers will listen. I am a firm believer that most people are not going to prevent you from doing something that benefits the business and, thus, helps them and you. If you have never had this conversation before and you are just beginning your career, just remember that having ideas and sharing them is a great thing. Not every idea that you propose is going to be accepted by everyone, sometimes for good reasons and sometimes for bad reasons. Not trying is what holds you back.

I went to a party hosted by one of the rapidly growing recruitment agencies in London. Within the first fifteen minutes I was introduced to an associate who had graduated just a couple of years back from a very prestigious Big Name University in the UK. We exchanged the usual topics of what we do and where we were from originally. Since my life and work experience covers four countries, the question of "where are you from" makes a great cocktail party conversation. It also offers an opportunity for people to relate if they have similar goals in mind. I learned that this woman was seriously considering moving from London to New York. Not only was she considering it, but she had already boldly proposed to the agency that she would open up an office in New York and bring in a new source of revenue for the business. Now, talk about moving out to move up. What a great move for a person at any career level, not just for someone who is a recent grad and is looking to create a bigger role for herself. This kind of a transfer will be an amazing opportunity for her to become an entrepreneur for a young growing business, to build something from scratch, and, at the same time, to experience life in a new country.

The concept of moving up for me is to feel like you are making progress. It can't be measured only in a more attractive business title or in a larger number of direct reports. As long as it is a meaningful opportunity for you and you feel like you are learning and advancing your career, it's progress, and that's what you should extract from your move.

Let's come back to Claire's story. Several years ago, she made a decision to move from China to Australia. Since we first met in 2007, we had a number of conversations about whether one has to be really brave to uproot oneself and one's family to move to a completely different environment. How quickly would you adjust? How scary would it be at first? At that time I only had my first Big Move experience, from Ukraine straight to the heart of Silicon Valley, without any prior travelling experience abroad (travel from Ukraine to Russia in Soviet times doesn't really count as being abroad). Claire was fascinated with the fact that I just went for it and never had any regrets.

I vividly remember we were having a discussion about whether she would ever want to take a huge risk in making an international move like that or whether it would even be the right thing for her, given the fact that she was a parent and has a very different level of responsibility, something that I can't even imagine how to cope with. Location was something that mattered to her a lot. It had to be a place where her son could be completely immersed into an English-speaking environment but also where both of them could still have access to the Chinese community.

When an opportunity came up to transition from focusing on operations in China to running a sales operation for the broader APAC region from Melbourne, Claire didn't immediately make a decision. We all need different amounts of time and push to make a leap. If someone told Claire back in 2007 that she was going to make such a drastic change to her lifestyle in just a couple of years, she probably would not have believed it. She thought about the possibilities, weighed pros and cons, and recognized that this was something that was going to bring her one step closer to her aspirations of working on a regional level in APAC, not on a country level. Claire was looking at an opportunity at running operations for a bigger team, larger revenues, and learning firsthand about channel and direct sales relationships across the region.

The alternative would have been to spend time looking for a new company and a new job that was going to afford her the right opportunity. Her progress in her career would have been much slower and would have been fraught with different challenges. She had a few sponsors, including me, in our Mountain View office, so we made the move happen for her. Everything else was up to her. Claire made the move with lots of courage and found it very rewarding. She learned a lot about APAC, made new connections, and had an opportunity to continue working with U.S. operations while expanding her knowledge of international software sales operations. Overall, she has gained very strong experience that will be valued by any global business.

I am a lot more impulsive when it comes to changes in life, career, and opportunities. Travel always boosts my life experience. I can't wait to get on a plane. Now that I am in London, even a train would do to go exploring for personal or for business reasons. It's really hard for me to stay in the same place for a long time. I know that in all my career moves I will always need a change of scenery in addition to needing the usual learning, personal growth, new experiences, and expansion of responsibilities. Moving to the United States was a big dream, my big American dream, to put it in terms familiar to everyone. Once that was done, I really thought I was settled in California. Like Julia, I drew from my chameleonic side and fully adjusted to living in California. What was there not to like? Great weather, many options for outdoor activities including proximity to ski resorts, plenty of interesting tech companies with lots of jobs and career opportunities, many new friends acquired in only a few years. I was going to stay put, right? So many people dream about being in San Francisco or close to it.

Ironically, I didn't have any real experience in Europe. Eastern Europe living is just not the same. I went straight from the heart of industrial Ukraine to

Silicon Valley. My first trip to Europe was only in 2006, seven years after my first epic international move. It was a business trip with Cisco and it did something amazing. It opened up possibilities. The confidence of having many more diverse opportunities ahead shifted my perception abruptly. That week in Germany, the UK, and a subsequent quick holiday escape to Paris for the weekend gave me a truly life-changing experience. I was hooked on the dream of globe-trotting. The American dream was just not going to be enough. I switched jobs within a few months to get into a smaller company, making sure that an international reach potential was there for me to explore. I networked. I spoke to everyone I met about my interest in truly being a part of the global business and not just focusing on U.S. markets. VeriSign turned out to be the best employment choice I could have imagined. The term *smaller company* is really relative here. Most significant software companies would be smaller compared to Cisco's megabusiness.

I credit Karen and a group of senior managers in the Geneva office for recognizing my interest and helping me act on it. Without their sponsorship and support of my local U.S. management team, the transfer would never have been possible. This was such a perfect job and value creation opportunity. I had skills that the team needed and they had an interest in having someone with a combination of U.S. operations expertise and interest in further developing other functions. I would love to tell you that I had planned all of this in detail but that would be stretching the truth. I simply jumped on an opportunity to further build my skills and make them more relevant to helping our growing international business. The sales operations field had been my core skill set for some time, and adding running order management and credit control teams to them for "outside of the U.S." markets was a natural fit. In all respects,, this move was definitely a moving out to move up choice in my book of personal growth. I left to run a larger team with more diverse functions, dealing with more complexities across more time zones, and got a much broader view of the business overall. Quite often a move outside the safety of company headquarters helps you meet a different level of talent. It takes a very entrepreneurial and dedicated group of people to help localize company offerings, communicate with the "mothership," and build company interests in international markets.

Good things do come to an end most of the time and being unprepared can really throw you off balance. I knew that my assignment to Geneva was a two-year gig but couldn't quite see what was going to happen at the end. What I discovered was a reaffirmation that you can't predict and plan all your moves. I theorized about localizing and staying in Switzerland. I imagined returning to California and looking for another opportunity within the business or outside of it. What I could have never predicted, was that VeriSign would sell our website security unit to Symantec and many roles would undergo a rapid transition. My assignment was expiring. Staying in

Switzerland was no longer an option. The most logical thing to do would have been to return to California and decide what I wanted to do for a living.

Now, an acquisition could be good and bad for individuals who are not in the executive suite. If your parachute is not quite golden, an exit is not the most lucrative solution. Interestingly, the transition period is where the opportunity lies. When a $6 billion business makes a $1.2 billion acquisition, many things have to happen to make it a success. Talent retention and savvy post M&A operation integration activities are areas where we can find unexpected prospects. If you are not on the list of people exiting right after the acquisition, you could create your own opportunity. Again, this becomes a great value creation exercise. Like all humans, I have my fair share of fears, uncertainty, and doubts. I didn't necessarily expect that something was going to materialize from thin air just to fit my needs. What happened was the most natural thing — I asked for a job to run the sales operations globally but from a location of my choice, London, which made good sense for the business as well, and I was accepted.

London was always on the top of my list of places to go and visit. By then, I had been there enough times to feel quite comfortable and could imagine myself settling there for a while. Since I truly became a transplant in Switzerland, uprooting was a bit painful. Switzerland was a fantastic location. But the excitement of a new job prospect, having a global outreach from London, and the fact that the theater and opera options were among the best in the world sealed the deal. Returning to California to do the same job would not have been the same. In fact, location choice this time made for a more enticing career move.

Reach out, assess, and discuss. International career moves don't happen by themselves. You may have to do some selling of yourself. If you have a bit of luck on your side, your sponsors will do a lot of selling on your behalf. Don't get discouraged if it doesn't work out. It would be truly amazing if every time we wanted something we got it. There is a lot of competition out there for great jobs in great locations. You are as capable as anyone else but it could so happen that this one time, there is someone else who is a better fit for the business you are part of. Let them have it! The next one will be yours.

Location, Location, Location!

There is a lot to be said about your perception of a location before you finally getting there. Before my move to the United States, I had a view of Silicon Valley as *the* most international place where jobs were easy to get and assimilation wouldn't be an issue. My perception was mostly fueled by American business people who I met while translating for various workshops in Ukraine. Having now lived in Geneva and London, I have to say that as far as places that are superfriendly for expats go, both of these cities are on top of my list. They all offer a great variety of expat community circles, support groups, common language interest gatherings, and much more. Once I left Ukraine, I was fortunate to live in places where I didn't have to struggle with being accepted into the local culture, business practices, or communities. All these locations have so many diverse groups of people that you never feel like you are sticking out. I empathize with people who move to Ukraine from any non-Russian-speaking country. They have to fight harder to understand what's going on around them, create valuable friendships, and deal with life and business infrastructure issues. While many expats moving to Ukraine enjoy the dramatic difference in lifestyle as a first-time experience, it's easiest for those who are single and don't have to assist their families to blend in.

My biggest surprise both in VeriSign's office in Geneva and Workshare's office in London was the number of people who moved from another country to work in both locations. Besides the frontalier folks commuting from France across the border (something that American colleagues got very excited about, a different perspective on life such as a morning commute to a different country), we had colleagues who at different times in their careers moved from Sweden, Denmark, Germany, Austria, Italy, and the list goes on. It's also great to be able to say that while in London I worked at a British tech business which attracted more than thirty nationalities to a small office close to Bricklane. That's pretty amazing. The diversity of perspectives is one of the key elements of what makes any high tech business a success. London's tech scene is expanding rapidly. It's a great time to be here. We can all incessantly debate whether Silicon Valley has an enormous competitive advantage over any other location on the globe, but I have now seen firsthand that London has plenty of opportunities for people who want to create startups, work for startups, or work at a fully grown-up tech company.

To me there are two major things to consider when making your location choice: the first is whether the place appeals to you personally. It has to make sense to you, to your soul, to your feeling of what being happy in a new place means. There has to be a deeper connection to have a higher chance to become a successful transplant, something to hold onto for more than a couple of weeks. The second major thing is how dynamic the place is in terms of overall business opportunity and international communities. Has it attracted plenty of foreign workers before you landed or are you one of the early settlers?

Don't get me wrong, I enjoyed the diversity, the buzz, and the opportunity of Silicon Valley. There is also such a thing as bad timing for anything you do, including an international move. I got to San Jose, California in 1999. My Russian college friends arrived just a year earlier. You may recall, this was exactly the time when the infamous dotcom bubble burst. It was easy to graduate but it wasn't easy to find the right job at the moment we needed to. Visa constraints and very finite amounts of financial resources can make even the best location in the world less than desirable in a particular place in time. We all made a series of decisions that led us to where we are today. Despite the crisis, we did well and have gone on to see the world, have pretty interesting careers, and create wide networks of business and personal relationships.

Most of the women I spoke with when gathering my thoughts for this book lived in attractive international hubs: San Francisco and, broadly, Silicon Valley, Seattle, London, and Melbourne. All of them as well as yours truly hit the jackpot: not only did we love these locations for a variety of personal reasons (culture, outdoor activities, proximity to other travel destinations we enjoyed, overall lifestyle, access to communities we cherished, and great restaurants and entertainment), but also they are all most dynamic in terms of being prominent business and entrepreneurship hubs offering us a plethora of career opportunities in the fields that we had selected.

Olga's choice of Odessa as a relocation destination is one that appears to be off the beaten path at first glance. If you dig deeper, you will find that it's a city that started out as an international hub and had more diversity than, frankly, any other city in Russia or Ukraine back a few centuries ago. With the revolution, communism, and all, things have gone in a different direction but the city is coming back from a slump. Olga's passion for this particular city was bigger than a desire to take a simple, general economic conditions point of view about it before making the move. However, she did have a great intuitive insight: Odessa is becoming more and more a popular tourist destination, with dozens of cruise ships making it a point to stop there and introduce their European and American customers to the wonders of the old merchant city, the pearl of the Black Sea, as they called it, during the spring, summer, and fall seasons.

We don't always define our international moves. Sometimes the moves define us. They influence the path we have ahead in ways that cannot be predicted before the first step is taken. I believe in choosing the place you will enjoy, gaining an understanding of what attracts you to it, and then putting everything else together. It doesn't have to be a childhood dream of a location. It's good enough if you give it some consideration, connect with a few friends, discuss it, and then follow your gut.

America was my childhood dream destination. I always imagined how I was going to be successful, with plenty of resources available to realize my life and career plans as well as travel plans. I planned and plotted and connected until the path became tangible. My passion for the country "where I would never be," as one old Russian rock song goes, was real. Everything was going to be better, from my lifestyle to my job opportunities. Any road I wanted to take was going to be open. Looking back now, this was a perfect student mentality phase. Being young, with my sights set on education, I formed a view of gains, milestones, steps, and potential hardships to overcome. In the end, a great prize of a better income and, as a result, a better lifestyle would await.

Geneva was not even on my future-must-see places list during my American exploration phase. I never imagined Switzerland as a destination I would relocate to one day. This was true until I landed in Geneva for my first business trip to Switzerland. What changed me was meeting people who were doing their expat gigs in Geneva, people who permanently moved there, and people who were local. Suddenly I was introduced to successful and interesting colleagues who I had a lot of respect for and who were moving around internationally. All of them were connected to the place and loved it. This location defined my path. I gained valuable work and life experience much faster than I would have back in California if I followed my career track. It also made me believe that this did not have to be my last international move. There was a lot more of the world to be seen, many more career paths to try, and, most importantly, more experience to be gained that could be valuable to others. I felt like this second relocation gave me the right of passage to provide mentoring and advice to other people. Now I had more breadth in my business and location positioning.

London always looked like a highly desirable place but on the too-hard-to-move-to list for me. Before I started travelling around the world, I couldn't imagine how London would fit into my life-work plans or rather my work-life plans. Isn't it virtually impossible to find a job in London? I had a couple of external interviews and they led nowhere. Pay attention! I was having doubts even after living and working in three countries. Having browsed through various social sites I discovered that many of my former classmates in Ukraine and my colleagues in the United States and South Africa at some point worked in London or were in London at the time of my browsing.

Once you start focusing on your plan, you notice more and more relevant data points served up to you. It's worse than annoying ads on the Internet. Suddenly, everyone you talk to loves London. They would enjoy working in London. They have been there on multiple business trips and they are absolutely enamored with it. There is always that one woman who moved to London for a job/boyfriend/school and was so happy that she never even imagined moving back to [insert the name of the country]. Every blog, article, or news item is about London. There is nothing else.

Once I relocated to London, I discovered a thriving tech community that was way beyond the obvious and immediate opportunities to work for large UK and U.S. companies. If you have a career in tech or are thinking about transitioning into tech, the time to move to London is now! The amount of media coverage, support structures, government funding, business incubators, lean startup groups, various knowledge sharing networks/Meetup groups, non-UK startups trying to penetrate this market, and UK startups looking for talent all create an incredibly fertile soil for business and opportunities for you.

On a personal level, nothing beats London for me in terms of theater, opera, musicals, amazing shopping opportunities, access to a pretty countryside with history under every stone, breathtaking coastal views of Cornwall, and of course, the ease of travel to anywhere else you haven't yet been to in Europe.

There is something to be said about how things change once you spend at least six months at your new destination and figure out what the most important things to you are. It may be the most thriving community for work and friendships but if there is something about the place that you can't stand, eventually it will wear you down.

Julia went back to California after her stint in Colorado. She still wants to remain in the United States but for her, the only place worth living in for any extended period of time is between San Francisco and San Jose. The weather gives this location just an unbeatable advantage in her mind. As a great salesperson, she can find a job anywhere, so why would it be somewhere less convenient?

When I talk to Sandra, the weather doesn't really come up that much. As does everyone who lives in London, she spends time talking about the weather. So do I. From sunny Barcelona to rainy London makes perfect sense in her case. It's not the weather that's driving her choice. Opportunities to work for big brands are better in London; there are simply more to choose from. And of course, her husband has chosen London as well, so it's a great place for the long-term plan for both of them.

All of this discussion is in the context of choosing a location to work, earn a living, and play, of course. There are plenty of other drivers for people who choose short-term work exchange programs, work-study programs, volunteer opportunities, or moves to follow a partner on a nonworking visa. Our stories and views are about how to choose a place we would enjoy living and working in, and, most importantly, managing to earn an independent living. Find something that will always make your new location special in your heart and choose the hubs where the business environment is hyperpositive and job opportunities are plentiful. In this way it will be easier to find something new if the original move doesn't work out. Create your emotional and financial parachute yourself if your employer is not offering one. The experience you gain in your new location will most likely outweigh your risks.

Career Plan: A Puzzle, Not a Ladder

When I think about career paths and spending a lifetime doing something, my soul always fills with dread. Frankly, I can never imagine doing anything of the same nature for the course of a lifetime. Maybe I haven't found the right thing yet. More likely, as we go through life, our interests change, and having an open attitude to what we will do next is actually the healthiest of choices.

Trying to talk to my mom about her work was always very painful. I could never get from her any coherent impression of her actual work duties other than repetitive actions at a conveyor of some sort, loud metallic noises, dirt, and the nuisance of returning home from work very late at night, always looking over her shoulder — who knew who was lurking there in the poorly lit streets. She worked at the same factory for forty-two years in pretty much the same type of job. My mom was laid off a few years after she reached retirement age as established by the pension authorities for factory workers in Ukraine. I was actually happy for her despite the fact that age discrimination is just a normal state of affairs in cases like hers. It was just not healthy to continue with that lifestyle. She had no expectations of finding what you love to do, following your heart, or any other exciting prospects that today's career consultants discuss with us.

Now, I am talking about an extreme case which sounds shocking for today's 20-somethings even in Ukraine. The truth is that the world until recently was full of these extreme cases. Most people, women even more so than men, worked to survive, not to thrive. The old Soviet constitution demanded that everyone had to be employed and to be a productive member of society. Those who were officially unemployed but had "other sources of income" were prosecuted under the law and were labeled with the term *tundeyadtsi*, most closely translated into English as *parasites*. So long to opportunities to do anything other than the work sanctioned by the government. No one cared about what you loved.

As the balance of power and money around the globe has been shifting, more and more people in many countries are raising their expectations about what they can get from the world of work, what is considered to be a failure, and how to build different careers during one's lifetime. We live in the best times for open opportunities everywhere we look and it would be a waste not to explore them!

Moving abroad is an amazing way to progress your career and your thinking and open up a whole new world of options. It also encourages us out of our comfort zones, pushes us to explore, and almost automatically enrolls us into Generation Flux. I stumbled upon Robert Safian's article about Generation Flux, which speaks of people who have multiple careers, sometimes from completely different fields, people who take risks and who are not afraid of getting fired or failure in general. This makes so much more sense to me than classic generation stereotypes. I can't say I personally share the values of Gen Xs or Millenials. Living in different countries challenges you and starts blurring generational boundaries. Your country's definition for generations also may not match standard American views. Life abroad makes you more accepting of constant change and the need to adapt. It also gives you new ways of approaching your own personal development and gaining new skills. As a result, you may just have to explore new career tracks. It's harder to stay within the course that you may have imagined from a particular location fifteen years ago.

The women who San Jose State University brought back together at the verge of the dotcom bust and I have one big Generation Flux start in common. We all were trained to be teachers of English as a second language and translators in Ukraine and Russia. By taking a step towards getting an MBA and moving to the United States, we got our Generation Flux admission ticket. Our teaching and translating career phases were over and our move to business began. Now that's where it becomes more complicated.

It took Olga eleven years of consistent marketing experience working for corporates of various sizes and PR work in three countries to realize that what she really wanted to do was to start her own business. All her accumulated experience brought her to a new level of awareness. Ekaterina has now happily spent twelve years in marketing and consulting work and is evaluating her options, including potential business development and partnership roles. Julia was in sales, sales specialist roles, and sales management and determined that she loved actual sales engagements most of all. She is also the most consistent of us in terms of the choice of her location and the industry she wants. Now, what makes her a perfect Generation Flux representative is that she also dabbled in writing, worked on an environmental website, and helped her mother sell her artisanal works online.

Once my MBA was done, I considered the teaching career to be over. I did a bit of sales, a bit of marketing, and then found myself to be pretty good at operations. It's all that stuff that takes a lot of attention, many hours of learning to become an expert, and a lot of effort to build efficient teams. When I started on the operations track ten years ago, my plan was to stay with it. What changed was the type of operations, industry segments, and company sizes, from hardware and financing to software, from leasing operations to sales operations, and, later, commercial operations. All were variations on a theme that required putting knowledge blocks together to understand the business foundation. The pivotal conversation about careers with Brian at the start of my VeriSign career phase helped me map out what I felt success would mean to me at that time. It meant getting to an executive level of responsibility to work in operations, but with a strategic view in the next seven years. Perfect, isn't it? It was all figured out until, in 2013, I felt like I finished a ten-year run, worked in many areas of operations, but hadn't really gotten the sense of accomplishment I imagined. Something was missing.

While I was working on this book, I also started my expat and executive coaching business so that I can help others who are seeking to find their global paths and improve their personal and team performance. Making these stories and thoughts available to other women who wish to peek into international career-minded people's histories is certainly one area of focus for 2014 for me. Another big interest for me is to go back to my career roots. There was a lot about teaching that I enjoyed. Skills acquired in that profession helped me become a better manager and teach relevant skills to others in the corporate world. While I am developing my Moving Without Shaking business, one place where I know for a fact that these teaching skills will be useful is in volunteering in women's empowerment programs. To combine teaching with my love of new countries and to experience more of a short-term stay opportunity rather than being a tourist, I have signed up to two volunteering programs in Tanzania. We will see where this puzzle piece takes me. It will certainly help me give back to communities in need and at the same time get some real experience helping people who are going through a similar decision-making process about meaning and purpose regarding their international careers.

Alexandra's career has been quite an interesting puzzle as well. She loves tech. Her studies have been in telecom. Her strengths are on both the technical side and the management relations side. Having worked for a number of big telecoms and run complex projects, she is arriving at a decision point. Previously, job availability and locations were driving her choices. France was great for education and getting started. Poland could probably now offer a faster move into a management or higher impact role overall. Alexandra said that many people are coming back to Poland for bigger management roles after they gain education and experience abroad. She enjoys London a lot more at this stage and is building her life here. Career is important but there is no rush to create a specific and immediate plan for growth. She has plenty of certifications to let her do what she does very well for IT projects and complex deployments. Alexandra is open to the future, which may include an MBA program in one of the best schools in the UK or skipping an MBA all together and becoming an entrepreneur on her own.

What I am trying to illustrate is that our priorities and interests change throughout our lives. When we build careers internationally, there are even more moving parts. Don't be afraid of what you may perceive as lateral moves or steps back. As long as the job you are taking is teaching you new skills, helping you meet great people to work with, or satisfying your search for happiness, career balance, or improvement, go for it. It doesn't matter what comes first, location choice, or career choice. The puzzle will come together piece by piece. It's how you create your personal brand out of that puzzle, how you tell your story across countries and continents, schools and education programs, jobs and companies, that is going to make you more marketable anywhere in the world.

Negotiating Your Move

Your location is chosen, your mind is set, the bosses are convinced, you are packing your bags…. Wait, what, when, and how are you going to be paid when you land in your host country? I personally don't like the term *host* as it contradicts my favorite term for relocations, transplantation that requires full immersion in the place you are moving to. For the sake of expat assignment contract terminology, in this chapter, let's talk about "home" country as the place you are leaving and the "host" country as the place you are moving to.

If you are one of the lucky souls, deservedly so, who secured an offer to move within the business, you already are miles ahead financially of student movers, people relocating on their own to just get a job, people moving toward a dream job to a new company, or those who are following their significant others. You will most likely be presented with an assignment agreement that spells out all the basics and a little more. Understanding what your company is offering and gently pushing the envelope toward the "more" side is what we need to talk about.

When you do your first big international move, the excitement is really hard to contain. When I was relocating to the United States as a student, all I had was a plane ticket and $600 in my wallet, with $550 of it already allocated to be spent on the first month of board and lodging (a great deal for the heart of Silicon Valley even in 1999, by the way!). I still remember that elated feeling, "I can't believe how lucky I am …. It's finally happening …. A one-way ticket, one-way ticket!" Truth be told, every time I moved to a new country I felt like I was a kid going on my first ever trip: excited, scared, and open to possibilities. It's pretty addictive to be able to relive that. Going places as a tourist or a business visitor is just not the same anymore; it's still great fun but doesn't give me the same adrenaline rush.

Let's assume you are not a student and your international move is an expat assignment. You will have all the same excitement with a lot less financial stress. "I can't believe how lucky I am …. It's finally happening …. One-way ticket …. Oh, wait, but I will need to go home to see friends, family, take care of stuff; who will pay for that? Surely the company should pay for it?" See how this goes? Thinking through the details of what you need covered and asking for them will not take the wind out of your sails. And no, your manager is not going to change her mind just because you are asking all these annoying detailed questions. No one will be challenging your commitment to the move, to the role, or to the company. You owe it to yourself to get the best deal possible. After all, you are the one disrupting your current life. You will greatly benefit from the decision but so will the company. At the end of the day, the business has more funds to support you through this move than you do, so don't be afraid to ask for a fair compensation package in exchange for your skills, commitment, and desire to take on the risk.

The big difference between my move to study and a much later move to work as an expat was that I had something to lose. It's easier to be brave relocating abroad when you are looking at prospects for gains from any point of view: experience, opportunity, first-time-in-your-life international travel, and a tremendous increase in your earnings potential. After all, you cannot possibly be worse off financially if you didn't have any savings to start with. Well, I take it back. In the United States, you can end up with a lot of debt post graduation. So you can be worse off in the short term.

Now, when you are beyond just starting out and have built yourself a career, there are so many more things to consider. Is your take-home pay going to be about the same or better? What about the living standard? Things cost different amounts in your host country's local currency than what you expect to see at home, and it's often not just an exchange rate difference. Can you afford the same type of accommodation? What about a car? Or would you have to change back to public transportation (oh no, I haven't done that since I was a kid!)?

Make a list of questions related to the offer and go through them with your relocation specialist one by one. Depending on your business size, you may find that there is a whole team dealing with moving people between various domestic and international locations and you will be in good hands with someone who has helped others numerous times. Quite often, companies retain a third party to deal with payments to you as well as various perks and benefits. Get the contacts and you will be helped promptly in cases of emergencies or other issues you may have.

What can you ask for? Well, pretty much anything that is important that makes your stay comfortable.

You are not necessarily going to get everything you request, like in any negotiation, but it's best to be educated about key elements before you go far into the process. The relocation team, if you are dealing with one, is an intermediary. Your boss ultimately is the person who holds the key to the budget and will have to work behind the scenes to agree on how much your skills and expertise are worth abroad.

Let's look at a few items that everyone should address when reviewing a relocation agreement, which may also be known as an international assignment agreement. The objective is to relocate you from your home country to your host country within the same company. If you truly want a professional opinion, get advice from an employment lawyer! While you are deciding on whether to seek legal opinion, here is my list of things to understand well before signing up.

- Salary and Benefits

Get clarity on whether your salary remains the same or gets adjusted to the host country's standards. It can go up or down, depending on where you are moving to and where you are coming from. Which payroll are you going to be on, both the home and host country's or just the home country's?

What other benefits can your employer offer in addition to your salary if you are moving to a more expensive location? Can they offer a housing allowance, a cost of living allowance, a transportation allowance?

Immigration services and advice get very expensive in many locations. It is customary for your employer to cover all of the relevant fees for you and your family. Make sure you understand what type of visa you are getting and get the most flexible one. You may decide to stay in the host country after the assignment ends. It would be prudent to ensure that your visa contributes to any long-term stay parameters that may exist in your destination. However, you may be stuck with having to go with whatever is available, so find out, understand, and move on.

If you are relocating with children, will the company pay for them to go to a private school? Perhaps the local educational system of your host country is great or perhaps it's subpar compared to what you are used to. The education system is something that is worth researching early on in the process. School fees can have a major impact on your disposable income.

What kind of medical, dental, and vision insurance do you currently have from your employer and does it change to accommodate your living abroad? Never underestimate the chance of a medical emergency and how expensive medical procedures can be in a host country; such expenses in your home country may normally be covered or may even be free.

- Taxes

Even in the times of Daniel Defoe and Benjamin Franklin, taxes were a certain thing. You will most certainly have to pay taxes but make sure you understand the structure of your contract and whether the company is going to provide you with a tax equalization scheme. What you will need is good advice from a tax professional on what you will owe, what the company funds, what part of your compensation is taxable in which country, and whether you are made whole in terms of your net take-home pay once all the reconciliations are made. Find out if your business is going to appoint a tax advisor for you and who will be responsible for paying for the services. If you haven't been given an offer to cover the expenses for a tax advisor, ask for it. Tax advice will most likely get expensive and confusing. I am certain of that!

If your company is generous with equity stakes, stock options, restricted stock units, or any other share type of compensation packages, definitely seek advice on vesting schemes, tax assessment timing, and how to represent these data to both countries' tax authorities. The great news is you are getting more money and perhaps a lottery ticket; the bad news is you have to understand and plan tax events so you are not caught off guard.

- Paid Time Off

Should you care about it? We live in times when many of us don't even bother taking our whole annual leave. Take it from a recovering workaholic, yes, you should care! Even if you don't take all of your days off, which I don't personally recommend (you are in your dream location after all, go explore!), at least you will get extra days paid out. That's money, too.

I have gone from having two months of holiday in the summer while teaching at a university in Ukraine to three weeks of leave in California. This didn't really matter much since I never was able to afford to do anything exciting over the course of those two months. Moving to Switzerland where people had five weeks of PTO made me understand why American colleagues always joked about Europeans being constantly away on holidays. Those two weeks extra do make a huge difference, trust me. You can actually have a two-week vacation at a time without feeling like you had to save up the whole year for it. Living and working in the UK as a local, not an intercompany transferee-expat, I have finally come to appreciate my five-week vacation allowance. Watch out for specifics in your contracts and use your well-deserved holiday time wisely to see your host country!

- Relocation Travel and Move

Packing is one of my worst nightmares. Love to move, hate to prepare for it. If you are anything like me, let's hope that your contract covers as much of your moving expenses as possible. What's there in the move? I just need a plane ticket, right? Well …. Everything depends on how much stuff you accumulated and what you are doing with it. Getting all your belongings moved could get quite expensive.

Besides your plane ticket (and yes, it is most likely one way at this stage), you will have to bring some stuff with you. Even if you are not truly moving your home and furniture, you still have to deal with moving your clothes, shoes (yes!), and any other personal items. Your business may pay for the packing and moving of all your personal belongings.

Now, where are you going to live? One thing you should ask for is a reconnaissance trip to your destination in advance of your move so you can investigate where you want to live, what type of properties you could get, and where your children will go to school. In some countries many rentals come fully furnished, so you will not need to worry about shipping or buying anything substantial for your apartment. What if you need the type of space that only comes unfurnished? Even going to IKEA to fill up a few rooms will be a substantial investment. Given the fact that the assignments are usually one- to two-years long, buying furnishings is just throwing money away. So go ahead, ask the question! Can you get a one-time allowance to buy furniture or just get a furnished apartment, a bit more pricey but less to coordinate?

There is never enough time to properly prepare for the big move, no matter how organized you are. Make use of local relocation agent services. Find out if your company is going to provide you with a contact and pay for the services. These third-party agencies are really helpful with quick real estate locations, showing you options based on preferences that you have preselected, and generally talking through the peculiarities of living in your future host country. They can also help facilitate the opening of a bank account. You will be surprised how difficult opening a bank account gets on short-term notice with you having no records in the host country. You may have to manipulate your home country credit cards while your banking gets sorted.

Depending on how many people you are moving and how complex your work schedule is, even with a relocation agent service and a premove reconnaissance trip, you may not be able to get the exact place you want. My advice is not to rush into a place that you are not 100% excited about. Some destinations have really hot rental markets and properties with good values for the money are very hard to find on short notice. You may actually have to live locally for a month and look for options yourself. Geneva is definitely one of those places where attractive apartments go very quickly. With a large expat community that is pretty secure in terms of their employers paying for housing in the host country, the prices are high and the timing and ability to accept available places quickly are really crucial.

Your company could make things easier for you by paying for at least a month (if you can get more, great, but then you are not letting yourself settle in quickly enough) of living in a fully serviced corporate apartment. Speaking of payments, make sure you understand what type of deposit is required on your new rental. If your housing is subsidized by your employer, you just need to ensure with your employer that the deposit is made accordingly. If you are paying for the property yourself, estimate how much money you need and get an advance if necessary. Your landlord in the host country may be asking for two to three months of a guarantee, and if you are like most of us, you may not have that amount of cash readily available.

- Home Leave

You may be going back and forth between your home and host countries on business fairly regularly. Still, if your employer is willing to offer at least one trip home fully paid in a year for you and your family, that would be great news.

Another thing you may want to inquire about besides a holiday home leave is emergencies. Hopefully an emergency won't come down to needing to be evacuated, but keep in mind that life is full of unexpected turns, so it's better to make sure that in case of any emergency, medical or not, you can at least have your airfare covered. This may not seem like such important advice for EU residents but for those of you shuttling between continents, this will be a good benefit to have. No request is petty. It's your time, your life is disrupted no matter how much for the better. Save money so that you don't feel like you are worse off upon your return.

- Exit (Termination, Localization, or Repatriation)

There is no other way of looking at it: if you are on an expat type of assignment, it will eventually end. Let's make sure that it's a happy exit for you regardless of why you are separating from the business that brought you to your dream location.

Termination of employment is not the most likely exit from an international assignment but things happen, companies get bought and sold, and businesses downsize, so be prepared. If the business decides to part ways with you, the least they can do is to get you home and cover your expenses. A severance package will depend on what the company typically offers and most likely your home country rules for these types of situations. If you decide to leave, it's fair to expect that you are on your own. Hopefully your contract doesn't have any clawback clauses requiring you to repay any of the benefits that you may have already consumed.

You have completed your assignment and you love the host country a lot. In fact, you love the country, love your job, love the company that has sent you over, and you really don't want to go back just yet. Your employer may extend your assignment but extensions get quite expensive. Whether this is a realistic expectation depends on the level of your contributions to the business. You can always ask to be localized, meaning you terminate your host country employment contract and sign up for a new one with the local entity. Forget the benefits and perks and get hired by the locals! You could still at least expect some assistance with immigration processing and fees, but most likely you will have to give up any other benefits you might have been enjoying.

Repatriation goes beyond moving you and your luggage back to the home country. What happens at the end of your assignment? Is there another job back home? I expect that you started the process of looking for a new opportunity at least six months in advance. What if there is nothing that suits you? Well, check your contract on what happens in that case. Do you leave happily after thirty days or later? This heavily depends on the locations of your move and the respective employment laws involved, but see what you can negotiate.

There is one more happy exit option. What if there is a great job available in a new location? I mean a new country! Have you thought of that possibility? Hopefully you uncover this during your search well in advance of your assignment termination. But that's a new contract story. Updated terms and conditions apply.

What we have looked at is the most lucrative scenario that expats could get, with most items covered, a secure situation, and a nice length of an assignment to get well adjusted to the job and the country. If you are moving abroad to take a job with a new company, which people who live in the EU do much more often than those who are outside the zone imagine, you can still ask for things that will make your move comfortable. Again, it all depends on your role and how much the company wants to acquire you, but you should always ask for the basics. After all, they have paid for your travel to the interview to meet with them, so perhaps they will cover some or all of your move expenses.

Everything is negotiable and depends on how perfect of a fit you are for the role and how expensive it is for the business to continue looking for someone else while they have you eager to move right away. You could work remotely from your home country first and take the time you need to move. Just make sure you are clear about how to deal with taxes in this case and any partial tax year arrangements you end up with. The worst thing to happen is to forget to file in either country, run up fines, and have to deal with even more bureaucracy as a result.

Hopefully jumping into all of these details and the thought of having to create a list of the most important questions and answers has not scared you off. At first glance, the list seems never ending, and the more you know, the less you feel you know. When I did my first move, I had no idea what to expect. I was a student and the Internet was barely starting, so the information was scarce. It was excitingly terrifying and terrifyingly exciting at the same time. When I did my expat move from California to Geneva, there was a lot more information everywhere but sifting through it was a huge time suck. I didn't really know what to ask and what a standard assignment contract would even look like. Luckily, I had a few people with experience to talk to. Since then I have had numerous discussions with people going through the same exercise.

After all, it's better to be prepared. It's also great to be in a situation when you finally have something to lose. Protect yourself from emergencies, understand the basics of the assignment contract terms, spend as little as possible of your personal financial resources, plan your exit way in advance, and enjoy the host country as much as you can.

Chapter 7
Relationships

Never Let You Go

Now on to the juicy topic, right? Enough of all of this stuff that we have to do to build our lives abroad: study, get jobs, look for opportunities, push for what we want, and invest time in developing personally and professionally. Relationships will be really fun in new places; why won't they be? First of all, a disclaimer: moving around the world and living in four countries doesn't make me a relationship expert. What it does help with is recognizing patterns, accumulating experience, and learning about what works and what doesn't when it comes to building and strengthening ties with others. And most importantly, after many successful and less successful attempts to stay connected, you finally acknowledge that relationships do require work whether the distance is short or long. Let's talk about how our decisions to gallivant around the world impact our partners, friends, and family. All these moves are for our pleasure only, aren't they? Or perhaps those who are staying home think of them that way? How dare they!

Those of us who moved abroad have lived through the anxiety of separation and have given promises to always stay in touch, always stay committed to communicating regularly and generally continuing to be great girlfriends/wives, friends, and family members. Then the move happens. Our significant others separated from us become more needy than ever. They email, call, want to be on Skype every waking moment, and refuse to "give us space." We get frustrated and sad, worry about how our commitments are perceived, step up communication, and then fall off the cliff again. My key learning from my experience of being away is that we must acknowledge that it's much harder to be the one who is left behind than the one on the move. It is even more difficult if you are moving to a foreign country with a great promise of exploration of so many new things, meeting people outside of your normal circle of acquaintances, and trying to grow roots.

What I am advocating for you new movers is finding a balance. Yes, we absolutely have to make more effort than our loved ones. Our lives are more hectic, and it takes a few months to settle in a new location no matter how amazing of a transplant you turn out to be. Our attention spans are getting shorter and shorter because of the impact of technology and multitasking. It is so much easier to forget your commitments when people are out of sight. The promise of never letting go gets broken on both sides of the equation. You are the one who is moving away, so my advice is work harder and be more forgiving.

I have a very good friend, Valeria, back in my hometown. We were extremely close when

I decided to go to California. I still remember how we were walking home after another day of teaching at our alma mater and started up a difficult conversation about what happens when I leave.

Now, this was the time when the Internet barely existed, phone calls internationally were outrageously expensive, and there was no Skype. I couldn't possibly return home often enough to maintain the relationship at the same level we had. We shared so many stories, hopes, pains, heartbreaks, and philosophies. In one clean shot it was going to be over. I was the one who wanted clarity on how we will stay in touch. My concern was that the friendship would be gone. My friend was very honest and told me upfront that she didn't enjoy writing letters or emails and life was too busy as it was for planning calls across time zones. It was an unusual twist since I was the one who was leaving and wanted to keep the connection going.

We have now been long-distance friends for fifteen years. We only reconnect when I go back home. However, every time we meet, it feels like we never separated. All the experiences that our lives have thrown at us don't really matter. We always enjoy our conversations at every opportunity. And, most importantly, neither one of us expects any different way of keeping the relationship going. You can argue that this is not a "real" friendship. My point is that staying connected means different things to different people in terms of frequency of contact and availability.

Diana and I often talk about her friends and family. She is very closely connected with people back in Colombia. Relationships make up a very important part of their lives. They are very passionate people, committed to family. Separation for her actually was much harder than it was for me. The distance between the UK and Colombia, work commitments, and travel costs make it impossible for her to go back home more than once a year. Her presence with the family is limited to two to three weeks a year. This is the sacrifice that she has had to make to pursue her dreams abroad. It's not depressing or sad, it's just the reality of choice that she has had to make to get better career opportunities and a chance to see the world.

Looking in from the outside, Diana is actually really good at never letting go without being overridden with a constant sense of guilt. Every year she books her Christmas holiday trip home way in advance. Gifts are a big part of her visit. Her family back in Colombia is doing well — they don't really need the gifts. It's the process of thinking about them, what they would like, how happy they will be to see her and discover all the little things she has carefully selected, that makes her return experience the happiest time of year for her, every time.

Olga is pretty good at maintaining relationships in multiple locations. Like me, she has lived in four countries, so it gets a little more complicated, as you can imagine. Her experience with her country of origin, Russia, and reestablishing relationships is quite interesting. I personally have not had a chance to come back and replant in one of the previous locations. My moves have always been onward and upward both from the point of view of career progression and how I perceived the new location and the lifestyle it was offering me. Olga's move to Moscow was also an upgrade. While she has returned to her home country, she was coming back to the capital, which made a huge difference in terms of job prospects.

Her experience is with three circles of friends, as she puts it: people who she knew in California, her classmates from her hometown, and everyone else. The group from California had that huge portion of their lives in common, great memories, and cultural experiences, so they didn't have to adjust to anything. They picked up and continued where they left off in California. Her classmates were the people who had a strong cluster of roots in common and long histories intermingled, so they accepted the changes that Olga had undergone in California, even peculiar ones like typing Russian words using Latin letters instead of the Cyrillic alphabet, since it was faster (okay, this was before the iPhone's international keyboard). New friendships with everyone else were much harder to form if people didn't have extensive experience living abroad: styles and attitudes clashed.

Sandra's story is quite impressive in terms of goal setting and also having faith in relationships, knowing that they are the right ones and will be there upon her return. She needed to return to Barcelona from London in order to get the job she wanted. After five years in London, she was finding it was still not looking promising in terms of getting into a position with an exciting brand. So she did what she had to do: she moved back to Barcelona where she could get the right experience.

The challenge was that she needed potentially at least a year of commitment or more for the move back to make sense both in terms of learning and the presentation of her CV. At that time, she already was in a relationship with her future husband. They were thinking about the future, planning to get married, so Sandra decided that the distance was not going to make a difference in how they felt about each other. On the contrary, it was to be the test that would challenge them but also serve as validation of their commitment. Sandra didn't take this lightly. It was a difficult decision but it turned out to be a great thing both on a personal and a professional level.

My first move from Ukraine to the United States was a little better than the moves of other Soviet dissidents in the 1970s who never were going to see their friends and family again. My move was still full of doubts about my ability to stay in touch as much as needed. Having bought my parents their first computer, I discovered that email was going to work well, at least with the family. They always wanted to get the news. Whatever format the news came in didn't really matter. The arrival of Skype in 2003 was revolutionary. It really felt like something out of sci-fi, both technologically and in upgrading my parents' skills. It worked! Free, always available, now mobile, it gave us enough opportunity to "see" each other to feel that the connection continued.

I fully expected to have two locations for the rest of my life and keep relationships going in Ukraine and California. Easy, right? The moves to Switzerland and the UK as well as making global friendships through working at international tech companies really overcomplicated this plan. Having lived in four countries and worked in nineteen, I was lucky to create many friendships. The problem of staying in touch got out of control. I signed up for LinkedIn, free membership at first, shortly after it started. It was 2004 and my focus was solely on my career. Two universities were behind me, so I figured that the best way to keep up with my friends was by using LinkedIn, a professional online network. All of us were careerists with different levels of aspirations. Why would we want to share anything other than job-related moves?

The arrival of Facebook didn't mean anything to me. It probably left me indifferent because I was not at the university anymore and only viewed it as a place for kids or students. Many of my friends asked if I was on it but I refused to join and couldn't see the value of a constant stream of updates. Who wants to know which restaurants I went to or what play I went to yesterday or what movie I watched and who I watched it with? Only while writing this book have I finally decided to try to recreate my offline network on Facebook. The reason I am talking about this is because it took me just one weekend to understand what I was missing. I am now a huge fan! If your life networks are clustered around different locations, companies, groups, and universities, it is fun at any age to be able to quickly look up where people are, see pictures, do a quick scan of priorities, and generally get news from your friends and family in under fifteen minutes a day.

The whole debate of whether your "friends" on Facebook are really friends is meaningless. Should you be friends with your boss? What about your boss's boss? Well, if you like her as a person, why not? Facebook provides you with the connection you need to keep up with people who you don't get a chance to see on a regular basis and want to be in touch with. My takeaway is, if you haven't joined Facebook yet and plan to relocate far away or your friends are the ones moving abroad, get on it! It helps keeping your friendships fresh. Nobody is forcing you to update your status every five minutes. Keep it live, engage with your friends, and you will not regret joining!

Another added benefit of a global social network like Facebook is to show you examples of what is possible. If you are dreaming about relocating abroad and your friends have just done it, or they have friends who already live in your dream destination, what can be better than watching their moves to inspire you to take a leap as well? Lots of studies have been done to prove to us the negative effects of social networks: besides stories about cheaters, plenty of people are reported to experience jealousy, envy, and depression as a result of seeing people who are so much more successful than they are. At least they think of others as much more accomplished. Why not focus on the positives? There are people within our immediate network or one degree of separation away who have potentially done exactly what we have been trying to plan. Study their moves, ask them questions, get their support, cheer them on, and you will get there as well. Find your source of inspiration, not your source of envy.

Are monolingual or bilingual social networks better for staying in touch with your friends and family? For those of you who are nonnative English speakers or live in countries where your government blocks access to Facebook, it's not a huge surprise that there are plenty of other social sites out there, alive and kicking. You have probably used one in Mandarin or Spanish or Russian. At some point I have explored Odnoklassniki (Одноклассники), a Russian competitor of Facebook. For those who are curious, the name is directly translated as Classmates. Even though it got started a couple of years after Facebook, it gained huge prominence in Russian-speaking regions and also across the global diaspora. It has also expanded into a few more languages of the former USSR and Eastern Bloc, Ukrainian included, and, then, a few years later, it went global with English. I am not going to discuss the viability of an expansion strategy of any particular network or the longevity of Facebook in this space.

We always are going to have to be where the majority of our connections are. Otherwise, it's not fun and the network effect doesn't actually work. Think of a creepy feeling when you are joining a new social networking site and have one friend only, or even worse, you are completely alone! I have to confess, it's really fun to see my international friends' updates in the core languages that I speak: English, Russian, Ukrainian, and French, as well as to peek at an occasional Spanish or German post and try to decipher what it's about.

The choice of a network so that you never let go of your friends in any location is a question of purpose and convenience as well as of time. Let's imagine English is not your native language and you would like to keep your home networks completely separate from your English-speaking friends. We get it. You could have plenty of reasons for doing this: too many English-speaking exes, people with careers or interests you don't want others to know about, or perhaps your dad shares really strange links and insists on being connected. Or simply your Russian-speaking friends who got started on Odnoklassniki are too invested in it and you can't move them off of it and onto Facebook. Then, by all means you will have to keep up with separate cultural and linguistic spheres of your networks through multiple accounts. You may not be able to change the way all your friends want to socialize and stay in touch. After all, you are the one hopping around the world and are not available for a soulful chat in the kitchen late into the night or a couple of glasses of great French wine in a small bar by Lake Geneva. Don't be stubborn; adjust to where the clusters you want to be part of are.

For English speakers I will make a reverse argument. Social networking preferences can work the other way around depending on where you land your expat gig or choose to go to school. Let's imagine you are trying to perfect your Russian and are moving to St. Petersburg. Of course, you will stay in touch with your friends at home on Facebook. I won't argue that you should abandon Facebook and only log into local language sites or try to convince all your friends to move with you. However, understanding local preferences online may help you create better relationships in the real world. Are your new friends on Odnoklassniki or V Kontakte? You are interested in learning the language, the culture, and becoming part of the inner circle. Find out where they spend most of their time and for what reasons and then engage.

I do regret not getting onto any social network other than LinkedIn before my move from the United States to Switzerland. I could have gotten a lot more out of the journey personally by keeping in touch and sharing with others. Many of these sites, beyond just being social, in essence are there to create a record of your own life. You have guessed right, I do like the Year in Review feature on Facebook. We tend to forget the little details that make our experiences so precious. The more things we do, the fewer moments we remember. A lot of experiences in these different countries which I was looking forward to soaking in so much are now a bit of a blur. Then again, it's never too late.

Whether you like Twitter because it doesn't pretend to create friendships but somehow does, LinkedIn for its professionalism, Facebook for its versatility, or Snapchat for its elusiveness, you will find that recording and sharing can be rewarding for you and your liaisons. If you are overly concerned about privacy, I can't help you. Everyone rationalizes what she wants to share and through what medium and what's public and what's private in her own way. You will need to find an approach that suits you best to keep the relationships going and be connected.

Actually, This Time It Is About Letting Go

Do you have difficulty in letting go of relationships that are no longer working? If you are like most humans, myself included, you probably do. Most of us don't like to say no to friends, family, significant others, spouses, colleagues, and bosses. It's not a surprise that there are lots of books written on how to say no in the most effective way and still keep the lights on in relationships.

What I have discovered through my relocations abroad is that putting a lot of distance between you and the people who are a negative influence in your life is the best solution of them all. What I am not suggesting is that you decide to move abroad just to escape. Escapist attitudes are terrible when you are trying to go for something bigger in your life that will require a lot more energy. Remember, the best moves have a purpose. Don't make an escape from a particular person your relocation goal. Moving away from unfortunate economic conditions is a great purpose. Moving toward building a more exciting future for yourself is even better.

Imagine you have come across an opportunity to move to a new country. Your package is fantastic, your life conditions are going to be improved dramatically, and your job prospects after the assignment are beyond your wildest dreams. You come home, have a discussion with your significant other, and find that the idea does not appeal to that other person at all. You now have a huge dilemma and you are the only one who can solve it. My test is to imagine yourself ten years from that day and then ask yourself: are you sure you are still with that same person? Are you going to regret giving up an opportunity for that person?

I have always moved abroad alone. No one could stop me or make me change my mind. The unfortunate truth is by making the decision to move under those conditions, you are, in essence, terminating the relationship early despite your promises to stay in touch, work it out long distance, and so on. Then again, if the other person's life plans are so much different from yours, do you really want to wait ten years to find out that you are not a great match? I have met both men and women who declined lucrative opportunities abroad to preserve a relationship. Years later they had regrets. Be an adult about it, have an open discussion to agree what outcome you expect. Don't make promises you don't intend to keep if you decide to move alone.

People are a lot less likely to share stories with you about when they actually chose to take an opportunity and walk away from someone in their life. Through all of my moves, I have heard a lot of great stories about couples that can live apart for a short period of time and then find a way to reunite. Since in real life both people in a relationship or marriage have to work for a living, I have always enjoyed hearing stories where no one has made a sacrifice to their career or personal development plan. The first one to leave has a more attractive offer, the second one finds a job as soon as it's possible or starts a business.

On my last vacation to Dubai, I ran into a young American couple living in Switzerland. Their story was a great example of how things can work if you have common goals. The boyfriend got a great offer from his current employer. The couple had a discussion and agreed that it was something he could not refuse. The girlfriend focused on her search very quickly and, luckily, was able to get a transfer as well. When I met them they were exploring the world together and thinking about family planning and where they would want to live when they had children. This couple was very mature in their approach and looked at both financial and emotional aspects of their decision.

Svetlana, a Ukrainian woman I met on a flight home a few chapters ago during our flight that lasted less than an hour, told me a very different story. She was travelling with her daughter, so I was curious if her husband was also moving. It turned out that he had no desire to live or work abroad. Svetlana was keen on improving their family finances and couldn't see him making a decision, so she made it herself. It sounds like a no-brainer when you get only a short glimpse into people's lives from a neutral outsider's view. The choice, however, is not just about keeping a relationship or making money. It's about making progress for one and the status quo for the other. When the attitudes of partners clash, a move together is not likely going to be a solution.

I have also come across a few stories from women who "almost" made a decision not to take a great study or job opportunity because of a stalling boyfriend. This type can be easily identified by incessant complaints about the prospect of separation, attempts to try to instill a sense of guilt, promises of staying in touch forever until the other party decides to return but, at the same time, displaying no interest in proposing his hand in marriage or planning a more short-distance future like a trip to the expat contract destination or simply a vacation in a mutually convenient location. His immediate actions upon the woman's departure may include a lack of communication via any means quickly followed by a break-up text or a Skype message. Beware of making decisions under pressure from others. At risk of sounding more pessimistic than I really am, I will add that our partners don't always have our best interests in mind. Then again, we are all selfish, so choose if you want to live the life that you want to live or adapt to your partner's demands, whether they are reasonable or not. It's your big move so you may be passing by an opportunity of a lifetime.

Negativity about your departure can come in many forms. We have dealt with the significant other issue, figured out if it was time to let go, then let go completely and irrevocably. Friends and family can also be pessimistic if their personal history and upbringing contradicts at its core what you are doing. It is important to be able to distinguish between well-intended comments and fears or personal barriers that people in your life may have. Letting go doesn't have to mean breaking up. My example of boyfriends, girlfriends, and spouses is the easier one. You don't have to spend a lifetime being guilty about the choice you have made; people move on.

Relocations abroad bring out a lot of demons we wouldn't have otherwise noticed. Let's say you are the first person in your family who went to university or moved away from your hometown, even to a bigger regional city let alone abroad. The school you went to as a kid has kids from the same type of family as yours. You have become very close friends. Suddenly, you go away to college and have these new aspirations to do something different with your life. Perhaps you want to volunteer in Kenya for a year to teach English to kids.

Guess what? What you want to do can be absolutely shocking to people with whom you grew up. Their plans are to stay where they are for the rest of their lives. Of course, perhaps they want to travel abroad on holiday, but just in theory, preferably if someone else could pay for it. Your new friends you met in college or during your first internship share your views and have similar plans. They are enterprising and clever about fundraising and making connections. The world to them is a welcoming and open place.

At the same time, the wall between you and people you knew as a child keeps growing. You don't need to convince them that what you are doing is right and they are naysayers. Letting it go and showing them that you are successful at any of your domestic or international ventures is the best way to handle it. You will never be able to convert everyone to your way of thinking or your set of beliefs. Perhaps they don't have any strong beliefs. They are just scared that you are going to a dangerous place. What if the only international experiences they have had are from the news on television or reality shows? Maybe they think that you are starting on a path that can only lead you to be broke, and you won't be able to build a life you deserve. Let go of your desire to argue about the benefits of what you are planning to accomplish internationally; accept that people close to you may have limitations in their views of what you can achieve, and go ahead and sign up for your adventure. You may actually expand their horizons by being a real, but not reality TV, person who is pursuing her dreams.

Meeting Expectations

Expectations, like relationships, are a two-way street. When you make a big decision to move abroad for the first time, to return, or to move again to a new country, you will have expectations of how relationships will continue developing and so will your colleagues, friends, and family. Clarity, commitment, and follow-through are very important. You need to play your part and people who are not moving with you have their roles as well. Since you are taking the initiative to relocate and impact other people's lives and perhaps throw them off balance, the burden is on you to make sure that expectations are set and regular checkpoints happen.

If you are moving within the same company, communications at work can be as challenging as maintaining personal connections outside of the office. This largely depends on whether your role is completely changing and if you are joining a different organization. Let's say you have a new and exciting role abroad and also have the luxury to continue working with the same group of people plus a local team in your host country. Easy, right? Meet the new colleagues, keep the ones you already know, how can this be difficult? Surprisingly, it may turn out to be a lot more complicated with people who you knew before.

Your established relationships are based on common experiences and rituals you have had, be it a once a week lunch, a once a month karaoke club session, or enjoying season tickets to hockey games. Suddenly, you are no longer available. That valuable face-to-face time that you have had is now reduced to an occasional Skype session and a team dinner once every six months. When you come back home for your annual leave or a set of business meetings, you only have a week at a time to pay visits, that is, if you are lucky. It's impossible to get to everyone, so you focus on family and close friends. People who were an important part of your work circle no longer get the same level of attention from you.

Relationships can be very fragile. They take a long time to build and a very short time to break apart. As the person who has moved away, you need to put yourself in other people's shoes. You won't be able to please everyone or maintain the same level of commitments, but you need to be very clear about what you are doing to help grow the connection instead of weakening it. Identify the people in the office who you will be spending the most time with on projects and propose a framework for collaboration long-distance. You could agree to schedule weekly or daily check-ins at the same time, making it a much more formal plan.

Why is it necessary? You used to be able to pop in and have a chat in the office, go for coffee, or catch up for a few minutes after work at any time. Now you need to send an email, try an instant message, or a text, whatever communication methods you prefer. Your accessibility level is dramatically different. You may find it frustrating that it's difficult to get hold of another party. They may even be more frustrated and believe that the relationship is no longer important.

The situation gets a lot worse across time zones. Working in operations, I have always found myself having to be available outside normal working hours whatever time zone I lived in. You always hear American teams talk about how many holidays Europeans have and how they always have to get up early to get on the phone to solve business issues, deliver training, or simply be in touch. Their European counterparts point out that they need to be available too late in the day and all the fires start and need to be put out after 5 p.m. Until you have experienced the reality on both sides, you may not see the other party's point of view.

Having worked for nine years in the Pacific Standard Time zone, I got used to the requirement to be available for a European team a little earlier than I would have liked. Before moving to California, time zones were never a challenge since my work at the university was purely local. I lived in Eastern Europe and time zone and availability issues never surfaced. After moving to Geneva, it became immediately obvious to me that the window to solve issues live was extremely short because of work with

American companies. These companies had core business functions and the majority of people who were empowered to make final decisions on particular business issues were located in the United States. You may end up having to work late or wait until the next day to get answers or the resolution you are looking for. This works in reverse, by the way, if you work for a British company with a big presence in the United States. Someone has to sacrifice a chunk of personal time. Having worked both on Central European Time and in London, I began to appreciate the opportunity that just one extra hour of time in the UK buys you while doing work with people on the American West Coast.

What's important to recognize for a new expat is that the time zone tables will have turned. You will experience what the local teams have to deal with on a daily basis in terms of scheduling. On top of that, the people you used to be working closely with most likely will be expecting to be in touch with you a lot. You are now their eyes and ears to help explain what people across the pond really mean when they say such and such. If you have often travelled abroad prior to your first move, this situation is already familiar to you as you have met your colleagues abroad and juggled your conference calls numerous times. A week here and there is fine to get the basics of working across cultures, but even a short-term assignment will most likely give you a new perspective. Plan and balance your availability carefully or the new expat job will most likely take over your life. For those workaholics out there, this situation may not be a very bad thing. However, those who want to experience a bit of life abroad, not just work, beware, and set expectations that you can meet without jeopardizing your opportunity to enjoy the local sights and culture.

Since we are talking about time zones, our Australian colleagues deserve a mention. I have always found people working in any Australian subsidiary very independent, driven, and self-sufficient. This can be partly attributed to the local culture but also to the fact that American or European managers cannot dedicate enough time to people based in that region. The best hires are people who can make their own decisions, follow their own processes that are vaguely in line with headquarters' requirements, and still make their numbers or deliver the project.

Let's come back to Claire's experiences. One of her big career goals was to go beyond China. She had her sights set on working with teams based in the Asia Pacific region. She certainly experienced the time zone disadvantage and learned the need to be independent. When you work for a technology company and things are moving very fast, you just cannot wait for someone who has not woken up yet to help you make a decision during your business hours. Moving to Australia from a small office in China was actually really helpful. She was now able to get to the bottom of the local team's needs much quicker. Despite that advantage, she still had to repeatedly work late to be able to communicate with managers and teams based in EMEA. Claire is one of those amazing people who never feels burdened by having to adjust to everyone else and work late if that means getting something done and helping her team. She likes being the connection for her local teams to the rest of the company.

If you don't deal with meetings in different time zones, you probably don't realize that Australia and California overlap in business hours. I never really thought about this until I moved to Europe. Europe was a great improvement in terms of working with EMEA colleagues but left me with significantly less time for the Australia-based connections. Skype, Telepresence, or whatever video conferencing solution you may be using is great. However, I am still a huge advocate of internal company meetings (there, I said it!) locally, in one conference room, when you are trying to build a complicated new process, roll out a new system, integrate one business into another, or simply understand a challenging situation or conduct a business review. There is a limit to how much you can achieve during a convenient time overlap. Now that you are fully aware of commitments, time zones, and work relationship challenges, it will be easier to take these things into account while juggling your assignment and life schedules.

About life schedules: When I was leaving the university for the first time, ready to take on teaching English just in the building next door, I honestly thought I was never going to be able to make new close friends. I imagined that I was going to be too busy to add any new relationships or that these relationships would be shallow. I'm really glad to admit that I was absolutely wrong! We make new connections when we change schools, neighborhoods, jobs, and cities. Can you imagine what happens when we change countries? We come across so many people who have an impact on our lives, our world views, and our future. Okay, that may be a lot more prominent for those of us who proudly carry the label of extravert and love socializing. I do hope that you jump into getting to know new people at work, expat circles, interest groups, and local pubs while keeping your old friendships.

We have discussed that our existing friendships and work relationships will most likely require more work and care once we move abroad. The other side of this is that making new connections will be as hard as maintaining old ones. It's not exactly like dating but there are some similar elements. For instance, you are trying to schedule a lunch and for months it just isn't working out. Perhaps you are running into a case of British politeness in rejecting you or perhaps both parties' schedules are just too complicated. Now, if you have a personal assistant, none of this probably even crosses your mind. For the rest of us who still have the luxury of planning our own lives, let's invest time into trying to nourish those new connections.

The more countries I lived in, the more complicated organizing a catch-up face to face got, even with friends who lived in the same location. A busy social calendar is not a joke.

My simple rules for success in keeping in touch and not being stuck in a new location by yourself, sulking about having left your good friends at home, are as follows:

1. Set expectations on what your calendar is like and don't sound like an I-am-too-busy jerk.

2. Make an effort to learn about your friends' whereabouts and travel plans.

3. Invite your friends who live abroad to stay with you when they are visiting.

4. Reach out to people yourself; don't wait to be invited!

5. If you meet someone new who you have things in common with, at the office or at an event, suggest to meet again for coffee/lunch/drinks/dinner or whatever works best for both of you.

Above all, make an effort to meet both locals and other expats. It's so easy to hide behind cultural stereotypes and culture shock. What's much harder but also more rewarding is to open up and embrace people and situations and get to know new friends and connections.

While dealing with expectations from friends and colleagues forces us to juggle a lot, family needs back home are the biggest pull of them all. A couple of years ago I came across a book, *Winning the War for Talent in Emerging Markets* by Sylvia Ann Hewlett and Ripa Rashid. Since I grew up in Ukraine, the country that is still considered to be an emerging market, I am always drawn to similar stories from other parts of the world. The authors proposed women as the solution in the talent war. I really liked that. Having met a lot of women from emerging markets at home and abroad who are breadwinners for their families, driven and ambitious, I agree, we are the solution for the employers from multinationals and for our own families. However, this solution comes with a price.

When I sat down to write *Moving Without Shaking* to describe international career journeys from women's points of view, I selected women who always had to work for a living and didn't have a real chance to take a break. They went to a university, learned a foreign language, took a risk to move abroad (some of them moved a few times), and found a way to follow their career aspirations. Not all of the women I spoke with were born in emerging markets but a similar theme was a concern regardless of where they grew up. The authors of *Winning the War for Talent in Emerging Markets* describe elder care as one of the strongest pulls affecting women's careers. For those of us who moved abroad, this pull becomes stronger the further the distance we put between parents who may be getting to the age of when they need care.

When we are exploring the world as international students, our parents are still young, have active lives, and have lots to look forward to and accomplish themselves. When we move as professionals, it is quite often later in our careers, particularly if we get expat assignments. With that comes a painful realization that our parents are aging and may need help but we are not there close to them. The difference between those of us who grew up in emerging markets and those who grew up in more established economies is that our parents still expect us to live somewhere nearby.

I have quite a few friends back home who spend most of their weekends helping their parents and grandparents. Very often the reason they have to be available is that they are the only ones in the family with a car or the first person in the family who has ever gotten a driver's license. All errands fall on them: going to supermarkets, shopping, driving parents to dentists, hospitals, or summer homes, widely known in Ukraine and Russia as *dachas*. The generation heading to college now will have an easier time. Not only is international migration becoming more and more commonplace in any economy, emerging or stable, but also their parents are a lot more economically independent and self-sufficient.

The topic of aging parents, particularly elderly mothers, came up frequently in the interviews for this book. There is no easy solution. I personally have justified my unavailability by the fact that building a career abroad helped me pay for things that my parents couldn't afford otherwise. Is it better to live close to your family but have a feeling of being unfulfilled professionally and not getting the level of income that you can elsewhere?

During the exodus from post Soviet territories in the 1990s, many people who I grew up with moved abroad with their parents. They were actively immigrating to Israel, Germany, Canada, and the United States. It was a very different story for them in moving internationally. Suddenly they were living abroad but with the support structure of their family. All the women who contributed to this book moved alone to start again in a new country with a school or a new job opportunity. Most of them still live abroad. Realistically, their situation is probably no different than most Americans today. Their children first go away to college and then move elsewhere for their first job, and then the second job, and so on. Living in the same town with your family is more of a luxury these days. The distances between children and parents in the United States are often further than what you will experience with your moves around Europe or from Eastern Europe.

We all worry about our families back at home. Yet we still continue on the path and with the lifestyle that we have chosen. Don't let yourself feel guilty about the decision to move abroad. At some point, if being back is what's most important for you and your family, you will return. Not everyone ends up permanently transplanting abroad. Look for things that help keep the connection with your family, be it email or Skype. Go back and visit as often as you can. Your parents most likely wouldn't want you to give up on your dream but will be very excited to hear from you about it on a more regular basis.

Chapter 8
Networking

The Offline World Still Exists

You have a brilliant LinkedIn profile. You have started mastering Twitter and now you're bragging to your less connected colleagues about a couple of thousand followers who, for the record, you didn't buy! You share professional updates constantly across all these media. That's it — you are networking! What else do you need to do? Everything is online these days. Who cares about getting together in a room? Well, the truth is, the idea of going to an event where you meet strangers and have to introduce yourself is making you ill. Now, imagine this meeting situation but now you are in a foreign country. You have just arrived and are going to a local mixer for expats set up by your relocation agency. What a pain! Who are you going to meet? Other expats? Or a bunch of local service providers who are there just to sell you more stuff that you don't need? Staying in the office focused on work is your plan. That's why you have moved abroad to begin with. Okay, maybe you will find time to go out with co-workers once in a while. It's also networking, isn't it?

I have gone through similar thoughts myself. For a lot of people the concept of networking means forcing themselves to make appearances at events on a schedule and not really enjoying them. We now have a great outlet through our global social networks to create visibility for our professional profiles and to connect with friends and fans. As an expat, you run an even higher risk to be stuck online in your virtual connections world, constantly looking back to the past instead of getting as much life experience and enjoying your new environment to its fullest. When you have challenging and exciting work, which is why we go for expat contracts, time flies by so fast. You can end up spending most of the two years of your assignment in the office or your flat on those very important late-night conference calls if you moved alone. Get out there and meet new people!

What's networking for you? For me, it's an opportunity to meet new people and find shared or aligned interests. It could be an event set up by a nonprofit organization, a business, a group of resourceful individuals, your own new office lunch event, a professional development seminar, or a workshop on any topic of interest. Networking is also meeting people you already know personally or professionally and sharing your latest big shiny update or signaling your new opportunity. There are an extraordinary number of expat associations, professional networking events, hobby, interest, and sports groups in many locations where you are likely to move. Don't overwhelm yourself with trying to do too many things at once, and keep an open mind about the outcomes of any event you are going to attend. I really love Meetup. It has simplified access, availability, and the organization of small networking events around the world. Branch out from pure expat events with your fellow country(wo)men. You do want to meet the locals and expats from countries other than your own. Trying to understand a new country only through the eyes of other temporary settlers who grew up in the same place is limiting. It doesn't help you master the local language either. It's so much easier to stay in your comfort zone, spending time with people who have similar backgrounds professionally, linguistically, and culturally. Balance different influences and inputs. If you have just moved abroad for the first time, push yourself to connect with people who don't know where you are coming from, figuratively speaking. Ask questions, show interest, and people will respond.

I don't want to underestimate the value of your local diaspora. You can find the services or professional advice that you need easier in your native language. Some of you will need exactly that at different times of your assignment. What I am emphasizing is the learning and the value that come from connecting with people who have different perspectives on local and global events, life situations, and professional opportunities.

When I first moved to California, I was very happy to immediately have met the Russian women I introduced earlier in this book. Olga, Julia, and Ekaterina were a very important part in helping me create my new life abroad. It was great meeting like-minded people and becoming friends so early on. I helped them with networking opportunities on campus in order to get them better-paying jobs when we were students. They introduced me to a large group of friends they had already formed off campus after their first year in the country. After graduation Julia helped me get a job when I lost mine and couldn't afford to be out of work for more than three weeks. They were my local diaspora, even though I grew up in Ukraine and they grew up in Russia. It was one country when we were kids forming our value and belief systems.

What we also did very successfully, individually and as a group, was to not get stuck only in what we knew. We made a lot of connections with Americans as well as with our fellow international students and professionals. We found a great balance between attending Russian-speaking events and campus career days. We talked to people about what we wanted to do, what careers interested us, and got referrals from other students and professors for a variety of jobs, projects, and internships. We didn't call this networking but that's exactly what it was.

Defining your networking goals and getting out there is critical early in your assignment abroad. The first-time student abroad, the volunteer and the business professional with a very busy international career, all can benefit from making connections in person. Don't give yourself a chance to be influenced by excuses that networking events are draining for you and you are tired anyway, people you meet are not interesting, and you can't speak the language to the degree of fluency that is needed to be effective. It's so much easier to post updates on LinkedIn or Facebook and hide at home instead of meeting new people face to face. We know that.

Start with a small number of events that you are really interested in. Think through what you are trying to achieve before going; this will help you not be disappointed at the end of the event. Oh look, this was useless! Yet another evening/morning/lunch I had given up for no reason! Did you attend to create a business connection? To look for a new job? To find a travel buddy or make new friends with whom to go to wine bars? How many people did you expect to talk to? Did you run into that one other Spanish speaker in the room and wouldn't talk to anyone else? You didn't enjoy the conversation that much but wouldn't dare try to talk to those people near the bar with their perfect posh English accents despite the fact that they seemed to be having a great time.

If you are on a two-year assignment, the time will run out before you know it. If it's important to you to meet new people outside of the office, do it early on. During my own two years in Geneva, I knew that Geneva was not meant to become a permanent relocation spot. It was a fantastic two-year plan to get experience working across EMEA and Asia Pac but, realistically, I couldn't see myself staying beyond the original term. I loved living there, adored a chance to learn how to ski, considered myself a transplant not an expat, but was very clear on the realities of the job market and the time needed for a new job search and financial decisions that had to be made. With that, I admit, my attitude was very much a seize-the-day one. I travelled around Europe by myself, hosted any friends who wanted to come over from the United States, Russia, or Ukraine, went out with my co-workers, attended a number of expat events, but I didn't consider tapping into the business networking or local professional development scene. I still got everything out of those two years that I was looking for: broader international experience at work and great friends from the office.

One distinct difference from the very first move abroad for me personally was much less interest in diasporas. On your second international move you acquire a new identity. It's a puzzle as to who you were when you first set out to live abroad and who you are after being influenced by your last host country. My friends in Switzerland thought I was very American in my views and attitudes as well as my behavior at work. It's not surprising, since my business education and experience came from the United States. My friends in Russia and Ukraine thought I was finally gravitating back to my original home country a lot more. When I lived in the United States, my language preference shifted to English pretty dramatically, even in conversations with Russian-speaking friends. They probably found it annoying but humored me. Living in Geneva, I started speaking Russian more often and visiting Ukraine regularly. It frankly didn't occur to me to specifically look for American expat gatherings while living in Switzerland. I did meet some Russians but it was not the same. Some culture diasporas may evolve differently in different countries. In some ways, I behaved like a typical expat during my Geneva days: too busy to look for new professional connections outside the office and focused very short-term to maximize the use of free time.

A side benefit of committing to networking events is better management of your work life abroad, that is, if you need to force yourself to at least create an appearance of balance. I have met many people both in Geneva and in London who move to these fantastic destinations alone and don't have commitments to rush home to. They don't have enough discipline to put themselves first or haven't figured out the looming possibility of a burnout. At the same time, if they still continue working with their familiar team from their old time zone or their new job is simply very challenging, the hours will expand. Before they know it, they have lived in a new country for six months, saw a few sights on the weekends, but largely remember coming home late, eating fast food on the way, and rushing back to the office in the morning without getting enough rest. Signing up for a networking event will become a great way of keeping yourself organized and out of the office or home, wherever you are working most in the evenings.

You may have moved to a location where your employer hosts a lot of marketing, customer, or partner events. Even if you are not in a job that typically represents the business at this type of function, explore if you could join it anyway. If you loathe networking events, at least you would already know a few people there. You will get to meet customers and partners. What can be a better way to build a local professional network? You will have much less pain with introductions; no need to make up something complicated, just tell people what you do in the business and where you have moved from.

One of the dangers of a fixed-term assignment is to lead you to think of your life as something that happens before and after the assignment and, thus, pause things that may be important to you. "When I come back, I will start." "When this is over, I will..." are the most typical ways you put your life on an expat hold. I certainly had those thoughts in Geneva. While living in the United States I always perceived that as a permanent relocation, so it was easy to create habits and continue with them. Geneva came with a specific timeline, so I didn't consider such things like getting a professional certification or taking a course at a local university. All these activities present great networking opportunities. Luckily I had a lot of energy to take on things I would probably have never done back in the United States like committing to learn how to ski and to improve my French by communicating.

If volunteering was a big part of your life back in your home country, there is no reason to stop when you relocate. Volunteering activities and events are not only rewarding but also a great source of new local networks. Research local and international organizations that could benefit from your help in your host city and get involved! Your causes may change with the move. Talk to your co-workers and find out what's important to the local community. Perhaps there's a glaring problem in your host country that suddenly resonates with you. Or perhaps there is an organization that needs their website translated or edited in your native language. Networking doesn't have to be about selling yourself. Help your new local community; your skills will be noticed and interesting opportunities may come your way even if you didn't specifically define them.

For the brave ones, why not start your own Meetup group locally? It's okay if you have never done it in your home country. What if there is a niche opportunity in your new location that no one has covered yet? You could be the one leading the way on the topic, meeting new people, and helping others build connections. Another promising alternative could be to identify a group that you like and approach the organizers about becoming a co-host or co-sponsor. You could bring a new edge to an existing group and build your network much faster.

Once you have taken a broader view on what networking is, you will see a lot more options on how to get introductions and attract new possibilities. Maybe events focused on mingling alone will never become your main source of new connections. However, practicing how you present yourself and what you want people to know about you is quite an important exercise for expats. Every event and interaction will require a different layer of your personal story. Do you want people to know how "international" you are? Do you want them to know what you do now? Are you working on something you want to share?

In my Swiss days, to answer that simple "Where are you from?" question, I would say to new people who I ran into in various parts of the world: "I am a Ukrainian American living in Switzerland." One of my Irish friends really liked that and told me that it was one of the best pitches he had ever heard. This gets back to the issue of accents and identity. People always say to me that I don't sound like a Ukrainian, American, Swiss, or English person, depending on which location I mention in the conversation. Then, quite often, I have to explain my journey in twenty seconds without sounding like a complete bore.

I remember coming up with this answer at a reception in a fabulous hotel in Cape Town when being politely asked, "Where are you coming from?" That was not a networking question but more of a very nice greeting from the staff. I said out loud, "From London today," and got the next question, "Do you live there?" and suddenly realized that my identity with a place, a country, or a culture was getting a bit more confused with every move I made. So I searched my tired brain and said, "No, I am a Ukrainian American, living in Geneva, in Switzerland" to get the whole story out at once and get it over with.

It becomes more convoluted when you are on your fourth location or more. Serial expats and multiple passport holders, beware! You may begin to sound like you are bragging and your travels are probably less relevant to the event or a specific encounter, too: "I am a Ukrainian American living in London. Oh, and I also lived in Geneva a couple of years ago." Not so sharp and snappy any more! This is probably not a good answer to a question at a hotel reception either — the people working there don't have time to hear your whole life story, however exciting it is.

In all seriousness, distilling your story and presenting it in the shortest and most effective way becomes very important for networking expats. The summary of where you live and what you do will be enhanced with just a touch of information about your background for your expat elevator pitch. That will open up more questions and before you know it, guess what? You are networking (yes, talking to new people at an event) without shaking. Now, practice that introduction in the local language of your host country or add in local idioms if you are speaking in the same language you grew up with and you will have no more barriers to a successful start.

Building Your Global Network Your Way

One of the questions I asked all the women interviewed for this book was whether networking was important for them in their careers and, more specifically, whether it had helped with any of their moves. By now you know that I am a big believer in the value of introductions and in sharing your goals and plans with as many people as possible. I wanted to see their perspectives on what building a global network meant for them and how successful they thought they were at it.

One common thread I have found was that all of the women I interviewed thought they could have been doing more in this area. It makes sense — we don't meet a lot of people who immediately claim to be master networkers. However, they all had people in their lives, family or friends, if not professional network connections, who were critical to the success of their moves abroad. A strong support structure is of tremendous value for those who are venturing out for the first time as well as for serial expats.

Julia said that back in the time of her first ever move, she didn't even know the word *networking*. It's true that we picked up this specific term in its current meaning when we arrived in the United States. The closest term in Russian, the word С В Я З И, connections, has existed for a very long time and thrived under the rule of bureaucrats. It implied exchanging favors and, most likely, acting dishonestly while doing so. Julia and her friends learned about networking and sponsorship in one go. They met a group of volunteers from one of the churches in the Bay Area while translating in a Russian orphanage. These people were so impressed with the young women that they wanted to help them advance in life and build successful careers.

Support came in the form of sponsorship to come to San Jose, California and study in the MBA program at San Jose State University.

I have already mentioned that the story of my first international move is quite similar. Without Jeff's sponsorship, mentoring, support, and guidance, it wouldn't have been possible. When you are in the beginning of your career and have very limited resources, people like Jeff and volunteers from the Menlo Park church become both your support system and lifeline. They are very rare and we are so lucky to run into them at all. It is even less likely to meet such people right at the time when we are searching for our paths. Having been on the receiving end of such support with my relocation abroad leaves me forever ready to help other people who are going through the same experience.

It was very interesting to compare how much emphasis we placed on networking activities and what we meant by them. Our experiences at San Jose State University were similar. After that, I would say Ekaterina has become the most dedicated networker of us all. She actually is a perfect study for my diaspora commentary as well as the person who branched out from the Russian community in the Bay Area very early on. She was very active with a couple of popular organizations just as they were starting out at the end of the 1990s, AMBAR (American Business Association of Russian-speaking professionals) being the one that is most well-known today. Ekaterina said that she got all her jobs through people who she met while networking. Every time I talk to her now, she is socializing, planning to meet people, planning to attend an event in a different city, or coming back from an event. She does acknowledge that she always invested time in networking and got results.

For Julia networking is making one-on-one connections with people and keeping in touch. Then again, she is a professional sales person, so besides her natural skill, her connecting skill improves with her time on the job. She is just getting better and better at the process plus she genuinely likes people. She is attracted to learning new things from others and enjoys the experience of meeting someone new, understanding their story, and sharing hers. Julia's networking skills particularly came in handy at the time she needed to move back to California from Colorado. She reached out to someone she knew in the Bay Area from one of her previous jobs. Her request was very targeted. She wanted to be introduced to get a job at a particular company. Her contact responded well because he was aware of her great professional reputation and was happy to refer her to the people who could help.

Olga's networking skills have continued developing tremendously after graduation. While she doesn't really feel that she is doing enough in terms of being part of professional associations and attending general events, her business connections are thriving. Being based in what we like to refer to as emerging markets, she fascinates me with her ability

to find the right people to help her provide high-quality services in the tourism industry: walking and private tours in Ukrainian destinations that are rapidly gaining popularity among Europeans and Americans. Her tours in the Black Sea cruise hubs, Odessa, Yalta, and Sevastopol (Crimea), are witty, flexible, and fun.

Olga points out that I have been living abroad for too long, so I have forgotten some emerging market basics. For example, face time is extremely important, phone calls are still a lot more relevant than emails for building trust in the absence of an opportunity to meet in person, reminding people of yourself by dropping by is valuable for fostering relationships, and making in person, not digital marketing referrals is critical to the success of a small business. People want to get more business, so idle chatter is a lot less welcome than real tangible opportunities to generate more clients or find new reliable employees or business partners. Small business owners in emerging markets are very entrepreneurial risk takers. They recognize business development potential quickly and want to engage with people who share similar philosophies. Suddenly, your LinkedIn profile gets absolutely devalued. The offline world really does exist here.

Karen values her business network tremendously. She has had great corporate jobs in the United States and met a lot of very capable people who built strong careers. Her first international assignment came completely out of the blue. Someone from a past workplace invited her to a new opportunity and she was off to South Africa in no time! Karen has a talent of not only making her interests known and taking risks but also listening to others. She knows what people's aspirations are, enjoys making connections, and likes matching people to opportunities. Networks are not thriving in a one-directional relationship. We have to be ready and willing to give back. At the same time, we can't expect that people will help us every time we ask and then get upset if it doesn't work out. Nurturing relationships and taking real interest in others is very important. It also takes time for the right match to occur.

There is also something to be said about having courage to just go for it: applying for many jobs yourself until you get one that pays enough, beating other people to a scholarship, introducing yourself to recruiters, figuring out the finances, and getting on a plane or train without knowing exactly what it's going to be like when you arrive. I have been very fortunate to have people help me in various ways with all of my international moves. The support structure was there. Yes, I had to work hard at it and view it as an important transaction, not just a frivolous move, every time (what's my contract? how am I going to be paid? what's the worst case scenario?). I also had to deal with the emotional state of moving alone to a new place. However, I wasn't really alone. There were always people along the way who I could lean on and ask for help to clarify all the things that were confusing, "foreign," and hard to figure out by myself.

Aleksandra impressed me with sharing that all the jobs she got internationally she found herself, with no assistance from networks whatsoever. In college days, her university had an exchange program to continue studies in France, so she applied. Her grades were excellent and, as a result, her acceptance was a proper reward for all the hard work she put into her course of study, including working on her French. After graduation Aleksandra posted her CV and started looking for her first real job. Within a month, she got it and was off to London to face her new business adventures.

It can be done! The location happened to be London, so while she didn't have any elaborate master plan, her career started adding more international building blocks to it before she spent a lot of time investigating and comparing opportunities. Having built a substantial amount of corporate experience and friends and connections in multiple countries, she is currently much better positioned to get jobs through her networks. Aleksandra also is getting into the habit of thinking about people who can help when her friends are exploring new options, jobs, and countries. I can see strong connector skills developing very quickly.

Sandra's moves are all around her family support network. She didn't have any business or school connections that could help steer her search when she moved to the UK. It took a while to get the type of job she wanted. She worked hard on her English and had various jobs to pay the bills until she won her first customer service position with a brand that was exciting. Her move back to Spain was also centered on general job hunting without having personal network references.

Since she has returned to London, Sandra has made some changes to her general networking style and has invested more in her LinkedIn profile, has gotten advice through personal references when looking for new jobs, and has generally improved her professional profile presence online. While she has found her way abroad and back home again while leaning a little on her family rather than professional acquaintances, the point is still the same — she was not completely alone. We need people in our lives to be there to help when we tackle big moves. Strong family bonds are great support structures for expats even if our ambitions differ. Something has to be stable.

Diana completed all her domestic and international moves as a student, so her networks were either family or university related. The UK was a big change for her; she was lucky to have a friend from Cali who moved earlier and was a little bit established in the country. Diana lived with her for the first month before getting her bearings in the new place. I find her approach to her moves and career quite practical and resourceful. She hasn't had the need yet to tap into professional networks to find a job abroad. Her work in the UK connected her with a great internal company network. She is highly valued by her colleagues and has managed to change jobs and responsibilities a couple of times. Diana is one of those people who is very helpful and builds up a lot of goodwill. Having worked with many colleagues across multiple countries, she has plenty of endorsements on and off LinkedIn and will always be able to tap into those relationships when she needs to in the future.

One of the big benefits of working for a large global American company is that people around you move constantly to new ventures within the business or get jobs with new employers. Even if you are staying with the same team or division in the same country for a few years, your network is growing simply because people are leaving for promotions, new locations, and different types of jobs, and your chances of leveraging those relationships across your industry go up.

Claire's big move to Australia from China was a great example of how to leverage your internal company network. She had a lot of supporters. People highly valued her skills and work ethic, so when the business started preparing different teams for divestiture, she was immediately put on the list of people who had to stay to keep the core business moving forward. Her office in China was downsizing but she could have continued there. However, the Melbourne location was offering her an opportunity to get closer to the team that was covering all the countries in Asia Pacific. What Claire always did very well was participate in global team meetings, ask questions, listen very actively, and also make herself noticed. She got to know people at headquarters and connected with them on a personal level. She takes genuine interest in everyone she comes across. It's pretty hard to be the only person who is remote when most other people have a location anchor and plenty of opportunities to interact face to face, or at least in the same time zone. It is wise to invest in travel early on when you join a company so that then it's easier to continue building relationships over the phone and by email.

Claire will never call herself a networking expert. She simply puts time into relationships with people with whom she works. She is attentive and respectful. These are actually great qualities to have when you work across cultures. Many things may not make perfect sense but instead of dismissing them, those of us who want to know why get the reward of being accepted by the locals, whether we are on a short-term business trip or a long-term expat assignment.

The most common theme in networking currently that runs through all our stories is the fact that we all have joined LinkedIn, added our pictures, wrote up our stories, and have shared professional updates reasonably frequently. When the network first started, none of us saw its huge value and potential. Now we can't see our work lives without it. What appeared to be a free gimmick has flourished into an extremely valuable service for which I am happy to pay monthly. It's the way we keep our contacts current, get matched to jobs, meet new recruiters, and find out more about our customers, prospects, colleagues, bosses, and former classmates. Six years ago, like everyone else, I was wondering if it was appropriate to have my picture on LinkedIn. "It's not that kind of social network?!" Now I get slightly annoyed when looking up people if they don't bother to provide me with enough information about them, including their professional headshot or whatever they deem to be acceptable for their profile picture (still no bikinis, please).

LinkedIn as a matching engine for jobs, contracts, and business leads is getting better. People are also getting better at using the service. Sharing updates raises your contacts' awareness of what you are up to and leads to business opportunities. The analytics piece is outstanding and keeps improving. You don't need to be a data scientist to get it. Any person who is part of the service can see the statistics through data that is easy to understand. Who is looking at the user's profile, sliced by the researcher's geography, industry, and job type, key words that led to the user, and the number of people looking the user up over a period of time are just a few highlights. This information is very valuable for anyone, but it is a simply extraordinary tool for expats. It's much harder to keep track of your colleagues, customers, and business partners when you move around. The network is still dominated by employees and employers from the United States, the UK, and Australia. The shift to non-English-speaking markets in terms of network participation is becoming more prominent. If you want to align your career or business in any country of the world to international job opportunities outside of your current country borders, you have to be on LinkedIn. The network is too effective to ignore. Even if you are a "passive" candidate or a business owner, you have a chance to be matched to interesting leads. Just don't keep your profile closed and invisible. It's like going to a major networking event and hiding in the bathroom most of the time so you don't have to talk to anyone.

The term *networking* covers so many areas today. Every expat can follow these simple rules: connect with people, show interest, learn about the local culture, and build global and local professional relationships. Join LinkedIn, if you haven't yet! Be adventurous; accept requests from people who you have never spoken with! Ask to talk to them first if you really must. It's all about getting to know people and offering them something of value. Receiving something in return will follow but you have to reach out and ask. I am convinced that you will find your own way of making it work at home and abroad.

In and Out of the Office

While remote work is getting traction in many businesses, we still spend a considerable amount of time in the office. Whether your corporate job is 9 to 5 (does it even happen for us expats?) or you have not thought about creating boundaries, you dedicate at least one third of your life to being around your colleagues. For many of us, work relationships spill

out of the office walls. Getting to know local
behavior patterns early on will help you be prepared
and fit in. What's expected? What's appropriate?
Depending on what you know and where you move,
you will need an adjustment period and someone to
guide you through the local etiquette.

I am talking about moving abroad as adults with
some level of education, work, and life experience.
Whether we like it or not, we have formed opinions
based on our knowledge of how things were in our
home country and, thus, we could be set in our
ways, just a little bit. Now, I am an extrovert, self-
proclaimed and confirmed by various personality
assessments. I tend to want to socialize, become
friends, (over)share, opine, offer insight, ask
questions, and learn about people I meet anywhere
in the world. Don't worry. I won't talk to you
nonstop throughout eleven hours of a plane ride.
You are safe. That's the time I switch into introvert
mode and either catch up on movies or write.

It doesn't matter to me what culture people have
arrived from; if we are in a situation that encourages
a one-on-one conversation, I will ask fairly personal
questions, but perhaps proceed with a little caution,
depending on the circumstances. I am curious about
who you are and how you got there. Remember
when we looked at natural curiosity as a condition
for successful transplantation to a foreign country? I
hope to never lose it.

Wherever you work, there is a community that has
already formed before your arrival. That community

has to have some informal rules to govern itself. Figuring out those rules is your priority, but don't lose your personality and who you are. You may feel like a worldly cosmopolitan expat or a stranger in the land of the strange, but I can guarantee you that there are plenty of locals where you land who will find you interesting precisely because you are different.

Let's imagine you have gotten over the level of culture shock that was appropriate for your specific relocation conditions and can now enjoy your office relationships. What are the local rituals? Do people go out to have lunch? Is it okay to ask someone to have dinner? Do people invite each other to their homes on the weekend? Is there someone in the office who always proposes new events and reasons to get together? How is it received? Do your colleagues meet outside the office at all if it isn't for an expensed meal during which you have discussed a carefully portioned amount of business related topics? Is it socially acceptable to have a glass of wine at lunch? Is smoking still permitted (indeed, there are some countries out there untouched by the ban)? Is the office generally relaxed or does it have quite a formal hierarchy? Maybe, oh horror, it has a dress code? All very useful things to understand so you can be less surprised about situations you end up facing.

One thing I would say is that a lot of rules and traditions could be stretched for you if you moved on an intercompany assignment. Local teams will invest time in making you feel welcome, introduce you around, and perhaps even take pity on you if you moved alone and take you out on a couple of weekend adventures. Or you could be lucky and already have strong local relationships. Then you have nothing to worry about in terms of discovery of local customs, traditions, rules, and habits. Just ask your friends before or after you arrive.

Certain types of professions transcend cultural differences in communication and socializing patterns. Not to stereotype (well, perhaps just a little), but sales people in the technology industry in many countries love to go out, have fun at bars and clubs, and want to win the achiever's club spot to enjoy the party experience to its fullest. Even people from more reserved cultures loosen up at annual events in Vegas. Don't judge the whole office culture by one type of job representative you work with.

When I left Ukraine you could still smoke at work in many offices. I know this sounds like it was ages ago but the truth is, the smoking habit took longer to break there. In fact, the first attempt at the ban was enforced only in 2012. On a recent business trip back to Kiev I was surprised to discover nonsmoking facilities, table football and Ping-Pong options in the office, along with an absolute lack of desire to show the buyers a good time by consuming copious amounts of alcohol. The office culture is changing with the times. The modernization of the way business is done is in progress. Now, if you move to Ukraine, you will most likely make friends in the office and go out for drinks. Coffee is becoming trendier and trendier, too, despite the absence of Starbucks. The local alternatives are actually pretty good. Equally, you still may have an opportunity to be invited to someone's small kitchen and have a heart-to-heart, slightly inebriated conversation accompanied by Olivier salad along with foreign delicacies from a local mega super market (yes, massive stores got to Ukraine).

You know that feeling of the first day of school? For the expat it could be a bit worse, depending on how prepared she feels at all times. When I moved to California, the contrast between in and out of the office behaviors in my home country and the United States appeared pretty stark. Looking back, some of it was probably related to living in smaller cities in the Bay Area, away from San Francisco. Many people had to drive fairly far to get to the office, so having a quick drink, wine, or coffee after work wasn't a big part of the culture. People work late as it is. They want to get home.

At first I thought that the difference was related to the time needed to become friends with people. Then I realized that most of the socializing happened at lunch. If people wanted to talk somewhat privately, but not formally in a conference room, away from others, they went for a coffee at Starbucks, Pete's, or a break room, which usually supplied coffee of fairly low quality. I never happened to work at one of those companies that paid their talent with free food on top of their salaries and other benefits, so all meeting arrangements were around either a cafeteria on campus or a local strip mall full of restaurants nearby. Lots of people brought lunch from home to eat at their desk or brought food back from a deli. Now, that's dedication! I am guilty of being one of those people as well, by the way. Ordering food to be brought in for a "team lunch," "lunch and learn," "brown bag lunch," or other similar activities that filled up well-deserved break times was also very common.

The most typical invitation in the middle of the week was for a team dinner if people out of town were flying in or if there was an event going on, in which case you were expected to attend. Asking someone to have dinner one on one without establishing a good friendship or relationship prior to the invitation always felt wrong. However, the time and place to get together where inviting co-workers wouldn't raise any eyebrows was a weekend barbecue. For those of you who are city dwellers living in cold climates, this may not be the most natural invitation to receive. In California, whether you live in an apartment or a house, there is always barbecue equipment to be found. Picnics or barbecues in parks were also a good alternative. Having lived in the UK for three years now, I confess the thought of organizing a barbecue doesn't cross my mind. In this weather, are you kidding me? I guess the habit didn't become part of my well-adjusted expat persona.

I eventually figured out most of the dos and don'ts of office life in the United States. One thing that I view as a personal limitation I had at that time was my perception of whether you should become friends with people you work with or not, particularly if you are in a management function. What's appropriate? In Ukraine during my teaching days I always was who I was at work. I didn't change my normal behavior. I liked being approachable. I said things that I believed in. I had opinions and I shared them. Early on the difference in age between my students and me was really negligible. I enjoyed being friends, sitting in cafes on our university campus and chatting about life, not studies.

Having gone through an MBA program in the United States, I had very little experience with the local workplace itself. The program was not just a course in management to me but also an introduction into the reality of life in California. Looking back, there were so many basic things I simply didn't know, like, for example, what a 7/11 store was. I had to relate all the basic elements of life, including convenience stores, back to what I was used to in my home country. My reality had to start making some sense before I could venture into managing teams in tech companies in America.

Having gotten my bearings and an MBA degree, I joined the corporate world with a bit of caution on how to present myself. I was concerned about being too different and, thus, too foreign in my approach to people and situations because I wanted to fit into the workplace with its traditions that were still not very clear or obvious to me. A few times I was told that I was too direct and aggressive without much of an explanation of what that meant. Eventually, I evaluated American office culture as overly politically correct and nonconfrontational. Now I would add that this was the case in comparison to what my previous experience had been.

Nine years later came the day of my move to Switzerland. To my huge surprise, I discovered that I came across as "American" to my European colleagues. I am sure it wasn't just the accent. Did I really adjust my behavior that much? Besides that, I realized that I was faced with a substantially different office culture and habits. I loved them! It was great to have lunch in cute little restaurants instead of the cafeteria or the break room. People were always socializing, planning to do things together, and actually doing them. To add a nice local flavor, in winter you would often hear the question, "Where are you going skiing/snowboarding this weekend?" If your colleagues asked how your weekend was, they were actually prepared to listen to your weekend story and share theirs in return. There were groups of friends, of course; that's how humans interact regardless of the culture or the type of setting, but they were not closed off at all.

This was my first "migrant" team experience where everyone had fairly recently moved to Geneva from somewhere else or was commuting to Geneva from France. People didn't necessarily feel like expats or talk about being expats; it was just a vibrant global community. I didn't get the experience of a Swiss office with the majority of people working there being Swiss nationals, so I don't want to generalize. Our community was more typical of many other offices in Switzerland that had expats.

While living in Switzerland I got to travel to the UK on business quite a bit. This travel made a big difference in my readiness to move to London. Not only had I a number of friends from different stages of my life who were living in the UK or planning to move there, but also I was very familiar with the office, the team, and the general office habits. How would I describe the social life of UK office workers? The pub is still at the center of it all. Meeting at a pub after work and grabbing a drink before heading home is absolutely normal and noncommittal. Don't feel like you have to drink beer (they do sell wine in pubs these days) or alcohol at all (mineral water, Coke, why not?). Dinner is a lot more involved event. It requires too much planning. A one and a half- to two-hour commute to work each way is not unusual. Most people live very far from the office. Who can afford to live close if they work in Central London these days? Going out to lunch is fairly normal, but I noticed a lot more similarities with the American office culture — bringing food back and working through lunch. Social events on the weekends are possible but require planning and some level of friendship. Business networking with people who are not from your office and casual recruitment and catch-up conversations have firmly moved to Costa Coffee and Starbucks as well as trendy alternative coffee shops. It's less expensive activity and permits you to block off shorter time slots.

Get to know your new colleagues, understand the socializing rules, don't be a stranger. You won't become everyone's friend but will certainly be able to create and maintain meaningful relationships and fill up your social calendar. Learn to read between the lines and don't get hung up on rejection or acceptance of invitations. Those who want to spend time with you outside the office will accept you. Be open to creating friendships at work, inviting your colleagues to do things beyond the office walls, and accepting invitations instead of using the excuse of always being too busy, and you will succeed in any office in any country.

Chapter 9

Attitude

Two Suitcases

We explored different elements that contribute to expat success. They are the following: building skills and knowledge through education and learning languages; raising your adaptability level to absorb culture shock; improving job opportunities by learning how to manage your career, network, and build relationships; and becoming an expert on managing your life long distance. We have touched upon the expat character through exploring the fear of settling. To wrap up, I would like to leave you with some thoughts about the transplant's attitude. Your attitude to life, taking responsibility for identifying what's important now, how to not be overpowered by setbacks and difficulties, and how to always look forward and plan for the future, however unexpected it may be, makes or breaks your chance at ultimate enjoyment of an expat assignment or permanent move abroad.

In the late 1970s my parents bought two big, ugly, fake leather suitcases, a navy blue one with a white flower pattern and a light brown one. This was the era before luggage-on-wheels. My parents hauled them on and off trains, buses, trolleybuses, and trams to get to our usual seaside town summer vacations. Everything that all three of us needed for a month always magically fit into these two hideous luggage pieces. Seeing these suitcases out in the middle of our tiny apartment always filled me with hope for an adventure. Despite the lack of comfort, I loved the journey itself and the mystery of an unexplored destination, as we often didn't know where we were going to stay, as well as the anticipation of meeting new people.

In 1999 I took the same two suitcases to California for my first big move abroad. What stuck with me was that everything that I owned, literally, fit into these 20-year-old icons from Soviet luggage makers. While living in California, I had accumulated stuff. When the time came to move, I had to talk to the movers, assess my belongings for insurance, arrange the packing crew to come in, and make decisions on what to donate, throw away, or leave behind until later when it would be needed again. Compare that with getting a one-way plane ticket and tossing everything you own into two suitcases. The irony was, whatever was left behind was never needed again, the stuff that was shipped later wasn't that important, and everything that was critical to live upon arrival in Geneva fit into two suitcases on wheels. My last move to the UK magically fit into two rather trendy and brand new suitcases.

I am not advocating giving up your material possessions or being extremely frugal as a prerequisite to expat success. Two suitcases became for me a metaphor for taking stock of where we are and compartmentalizing things that are truly important versus everything else before the big move. This means having an attitude of focusing on what you need right now and in the immediate future, at a minimum, to be reasonably comfortable. What are the things, tangible or intangible, that are going to support you as you replant in the new country? Things that you truly need so the move goes through without panic attacks.

You simply cannot plan for everything that you will need to have, learn, or experience. Leaving your comfort zone will happen very soon after the move. We have a wide range of planning skills and commitment to it, from nonexistent to moderately acceptable, except for those lucky people who live to plan. If you feel like you have an unmanageable amount of things to get through before the the day you move and are drowning, get more specific about what is important to you and why.

Make a list of what you need to bring on the plane with you. The rest of the stuff will eventually arrive but you need to be prepared to live without it for a few weeks, even if you are not moving that far. Does the thought of giving up your dear belongings make your skin crawl? I did have a horrible unsettled feeling for a bit when getting myself together to move to Geneva. I got all of this stuff! I don't know where to start! It's just a two-year assignment. My home is still in California, isn't it? But what if I need something? Actually, you really don't need anything that badly. Once you accept the fact that you may be in a temporary living arrangement for a few weeks or have to survive without your favorite DVD collection (if you haven't moved to much more mobile media storage yet), you realize it's going to be all right.

At the same time, make a list of intangible things you have to address within the first couple of weeks of your arrival. What do you absolutely have to do to not go mad? My short list covers living arrangement and transportation, Internet access, and registration with local authorities if applicable. The short list consists of essentials; it doesn't matter what your home country is and where you are moving to but you have to live somewhere and get to your new office. Registration procedures and visa regimes vary significantly from country to country. That's what your local immigration advisors or government websites, if you are a do-it-yourself migrant type, are for. I won't go into any details here. Let me just say that I have spent weeks of my life on filling out paperwork with and without legal help, waiting in lines at official institutions that deal with visas and immigration, including camping overnight outside of some of them to get in. Lately, admittedly, I have seen more improvement with appointment scheduling and applicant processing everywhere. Technology does help, no matter how much we complain about government inefficiencies. Have you noticed that Internet access made it to this short list? My first move to the United States was really just about two things: where do I live and how do I get to school? Fast forward to today, and I cannot picture being offline at home or on the road. If you are moving with children, school choice will make it to your essentials list; it just wasn't on mine.

Once these key things are cleared up and planned, upon arrival you should tackle the bank account setup, home phone, TV, a local mobile contract, and eventually, a local tax advisor. Make as long a list as you wish; however, I urge you to adapt something similar to my two suitcase attitude. You can easily get overwhelmed with things that you don't know and that take a long time to research. Would your minimalistic plan fit on a sticky note? On a phone screen? Okay, maybe on an iPad mini? I hope so. Narrow down what you absolutely must take care of and jump in!

What I propose is for you to learn how to let go of your mental and physical clutter. Physical clutter is almost always easier to deal with. Free yourself from accumulated debris of stuff and focus on the most important things that will make you comfortable with your move. Instead of imagining the longest lists of items to buy, find, sort through, move, organize, and pretend that you can only live out of two suitcases. What would you bring? Put a limit on the amount of cuddly toys, favorite suits, shoes, or books that you insist on keeping instead of moving your library to the Kindle. What if your old life was not recoverable, like in a worst case scenario, erased by a natural disaster? What would you most regret losing? What would you need to reestablish your comfortable existence? Being pragmatic about what is going to fit into your new location is something to consider. Are you moving from a large comfortable family home to a smaller city apartment? Or vice versa? Have you stored things in your garage for years so that you don't even know what they are? Are you leaving the house behind or have to sell it, get rid of everything, and move on? Don't take more work on yourself than you need to.

Mental clutter is harder to clear out. As expats we have to focus on the future but also deal with what we are leaving behind. Too often we spend almost as much time trying to work out how to move and what we are going to need as actually doing it. If you hate lists and prefer doing everything at the last minute, work with a relocation agent. It should be someone who can create a framework for you on what you need for your physical move. This will relieve the pressure on you to think everything through and plan in advance. My personality type does everything at the last minute. I thrive in a chaotic environment and make sense out of everything as I go along. If you approach things similarly, you can get caught up in trying to tackle something that is not feasible to achieve at the last minute. If this is your first big move and you have hoarded things for years, you really don't know how much time you are going to need to get through everything, trust me. While a relocation agent will help you with the framework, she most likely won't chase you too much with the schedule. You will have to deliver on what has been proposed, which is still better than trying to sort everything out yourself! If you live to plan, plot, and schedule, then the material possessions migration part of your relocation will be a breeze.

Letting go of things and leaving old fears behind is equally important. Our friends will not abandon us. We will eventually find a new comfort zone after stretching ourselves a bit too far. Things that were important at home may fade. Priorities will change. We are on to a new chapter of our lives, so let's get rid of habits and routines that are slowing down our acceptance and enjoyment of the brave new world of expat living. Make sure you take care of the mental clutter! This is what having a "no barriers" attitude is all about at the start of your move.

No Barriers

Moving abroad is glamorous but it may also be the hardest thing you ever do. It can be an emotional and lonely experience. There is separation anxiety, the fear of the unknown, and the feeling of loss of many things familiar. It's so easy to play the worst case scenarios and create chaos in your head. Don't build "what if" scenarios; focus on why you are making the move instead. What is the ultimate goal? Exploring the world through travel? Learning a new language? Making more money? Getting a career you always wanted? Following your passions whatever they are? Don't build more barriers than may already exist. Stop listening to the voice in your head challenging you on whether you can make it happen. Similarly, stop listening to people who tell you it's not the right thing for you or it's not going to work. It will work. You don't need to be rich or at the very top of your career to successfully relocate abroad. What you need is resourcefulness and a "no barriers" attitude.

When I first told my parents I was going to move to the United States, it was just a couple of years after the Soviet Union and the banks had collapsed. I was in school and had no income to brag about or live on. I also did not have a plan to make the move happen. In fact, I had absolutely no idea what needed to be done to accomplish my fairly ambitious goal. I vaguely thought that the move was going to be sponsored by one of the American universities that was going to recognize my genius and accept me into a master's program. I also had no idea what field I wanted to focus on in my studies.

One of the first things that my dad said to me, after I had made my declaration, was, "Your grandmother's uncle went to America before the revolution, did hard labor, got sick, and had to come back home with nothing. Then he went on to participate in the revolution and was exiled." I know he didn't mean to work hard on creating a barrier. Luckily I was not very impressionable and didn't even know about the ability a lot of people have to catastrophize. In my mind, my dad was just trying to tell me an old family story since there wasn't a new one related to what I was trying to do. There wasn't an imagine-what-could-happen-to-you part in this monolog. I certainly wish the conversation went more along the lines of this: "What an exciting idea! What are you going to do to be able to go there? How would you earn money for this move and for getting started where you're going? Do you know anyone who will be able to help you? What do you want to achieve when you are there? Why America, not England? Do you want to live there permanently? What do you think you can do for a living there? Do you have an idea about which state you would like to first move to?" Instead, what I got was, sadly, a depressing tale of the prerevolutionary adventures of my poor relative. It was surprising but then again I was used to people in my family trying to relate things to basic and familiar facts to explain the unknown.

If I wanted to start imagining the worst case scenarios for my journey abroad, I could have very easily gone down the road of catastrophizing myself: "Oh, what if I can't study in the American system? It's so different! We are not prepared for these multiple-choice tests. Or worse, what if my scholarship gets cancelled? I wouldn't have any money to live there. I will be broke. What's going to happen? I will have to come back. Everyone will think I am a loser. What if I get sick? Can I even pay the doctors? Oh no, I will have to come back! What if I don't have enough money for the return ticket? Everyone will think I am a loser." And so on, down and down in the spiral we go.

Whatever happens after your move, you will deal with one thing at a time! I did get sick within my first four months of living in the United States and had to have surgery, a real one, with a few hours of general anesthesia. It all ended up fine. I also failed an accounting class! I admit this felt much worse than having surgery since in my home country my graduation always meant receiving honors: any year in school, all ten years, as well as five years at the university. I hated those American multiple-choice tests after all! Give me a paper to write any time. Alternatively, I can talk about anything, too. So what? I took it again, passed, and still graduated with an above-average GPA that no one cares about anyway. Now that I have started my business to coach expats and executives, doing accounting never made it to my priority list. Solution? I have hired someone much more qualified and interested in the specifics of UK business incorporation and accounting than I could ever be.

A no barriers attitude is having the drive to go after what you want despite yourself and others. Overcome your fears by talking to someone positive. Find a mentor, a sponsor, a coach, whoever you find suitable to help you inspire yourself to transform into a confident global citizen. Please don't listen to people who come up with barriers for you. Things you may end up hearing have the capacity to instill doubt in the most fearless of us. "Aren't you too old to do this? Shouldn't you be thinking about your pension funds instead? Oh dear, aren't you too young and inexperienced to move abroad by yourself? You are a woman; it will be hard for you all by yourself! Why not stay where everyone you know lives? Wouldn't it be so much nicer if we can continue seeing each other? Why can't you ever settle? What is it that you care so much about abroad? We have all the same things here, maybe even better! You will be so lonely, won't you? You are single now; you won't be able to date in that culture, let alone get married! Think about your children, how nice it would be for them to be close to friends and family! Who will support you when you move? What if you have a medical emergency?" Focus on what you want to happen once you move, not on what ifs. Shift away from negative influences and wear your I-have-no-barriers attitude on your sleeve.

People will share their own fears with you. These are their fears and they are holding them back, not you. You are the one who is on track to move without shaking. Be polite and don't get into lengthy debates about why that one particularly horrendous thing is not going to happen to you. You can't win anything by wasting your energy on debating endlessly what if scenarios that other people think of. Make a plan, take charge of your own future, and move to your dream destination.

Jeff Fadiman, marketing professor who I mentioned earlier in this book, became my mentor, sponsor, and planner. We wrote an incredible amount of emails during 1998 and 1999. Technology made our interactions a lot faster and detailed than I could have ever imagined. In fact, I can't imagine how we would have gotten through the endless Q&A and all the things that needed to be taken care of in order for me to get the scholarship, become his teaching assistant, figure out how to pass the GMAT and TOEFL in one of two available test centers in Ukraine at that time (ugh! multiple choice and computerized!), get admitted to San Jose State's MBA program, and move to California. All that happened within twelve months, which seemed like an eternity of planning to me. This was also at the time of the beginning of the Internet and slow speeds. Not a lot was available online, so relying on and trusting Jeff was the most trust I had ever put in anyone in my life. He is an experienced fundraiser and well-connected at school. This was a key mentoring activity on Jeff's part: who to ask, what to ask for, what kind of paperwork to provide, and how to write an American resume. He also became my sponsor in a very corporate sense of the word: a person interested in me taking the next step, removing obstacles to my career journey. He made a case for why I needed the scholarship, why I deserved it, and why I was going to be a great teaching assistant for his communications course. When I think about it now, it never even crossed my mind that I might not have been suitable to work in an American education system. He has helped me reinforce my belief that I was going to be great at anything I was going to do. Jeff explained that I actually already was a strong communicator in English, having never been to an English-speaking country, let alone lived there.

All the stories in this book are from real women who have taken the necessary steps to get to their international career goals through studying abroad and/or working abroad. They all had some difficult times during their moves, be it cultural adaptation, financial matters, or long-distance relationships. What they all have in common is the drive to not give up but, instead, find ways to deal with the issues and challenges, alone or with the support of people close to them. They also all initiated their moves.

Were things hard for them once they landed in their new locations? Of course they were. I have even compiled a list here that each of the interviewees contributed to. Life throws hard things at you whether you are at home or abroad, on vacation, or on a plane to a business trip. It very often turns out that the worst things you imagined haven't even made it to the list of the most difficult things you have actually experienced. Here is our collective list of the hardest things to deal with as an expat:

- Language
- Culture
- Being far away from family and friends
- Making new friends
- Climate
- Food
- Setting up infrastructure/life basics
- Medical care
- Visa/Immigration paperwork
- Finding the first job

- Earning enough money to have a good standard of living

- Meaningless work

- Moving your belongings

- Studying in a foreign education system

- Sudden freedom

It's not a surprise that some of the things we expats, transplants, and global wanderers have found very hard also were the most rewarding in our experiences. We all appreciate mastery. We love the sense of achievement. It is enjoyable to overcome difficulties and be able to say that we have made it. Here is the list of things and achievements that we have found to be the most rewarding:

- Education

- Career

- Language

- Meeting people from different cultures

- Making new friends for a lifetime

- Experiencing a new country

- Travel

- Understanding the world in a different way

Studying abroad is hard but we value our educational opportunities tremendously. Finding the first job is painful but it's a start to a great international career. Language learning is a lengthy process but it is key to your new friendships and career choices. Cultural differences confuse us at first but once we learn the patterns, we enjoy people who come from different backgrounds and help us experience and understand the world in a different way. They are instrumental for us to become truly global citizens.

One of the questions I asked was about whether they, as women with corporate careers, saw any gender-specific barriers when moving abroad. Bluntly, being a woman, was it harder to initiate and follow through with the move abroad? I had to ask. I personally have never felt at a disadvantage when chasing an international opportunity. At the time of their moves, all these women were solely relying on themselves alone for their financial success. Did they run into challenges that men wouldn't have to deal with? The topics of women's empowerment, and women's representation at the top of corporations and on boards of directors are gaining more and more prominence worldwide. There is a large number of well-funded nonprofit organizations not only encouraging women to take charge of their lives and careers but also helping them through mentoring, financing, and education.

This book is not about women's empowerment. It's about empowered women. It's about nine women who have made their own choices and committed to building their international lifestyles. All of us have successful careers and didn't find it harder to do what we wanted to do because we were women in the business environment. You can say we were lucky or we didn't yet reach for the level where the glass ceiling would have been obvious or that the times are finally changing. All of our host cities were young urban communities, as one of my interviewees put it, and we were welcomed. There are plenty of issues today and many countries where women's lives are so much harder or plain dangerous. What I wanted to share here is these incredible stories of women "next door" who pursued their dreams.

On to the Next Thing

All good things, including your stay abroad, must come to an end. Is it really true? You can think about the exit, repatriation, or, instead, treat it as your gateway to the Next Big Thing. If you have read this book this far, by now you know that I have no experience with repatriation at this time. All of my moves truly were onto the next thing: country and job. Some of the women who shared their stories with me were very good with exits. They knew when it was time and they had a plan where to come back to. They had favorite cities chosen and their job searches planned out. Others decided to stay in their expat location for the unforeseeable future.

Your first move may not be your last one. You may or may not choose to return to your home country right away. The decision is yours to make. Many expats are disappointed with their lack of planning of their exit if they were transferred abroad by their employer. Many students are also disappointed that they only get short-term visas in the countries that hosted them to go to school.

What if you transferred yourself? You only have yourself to be disappointed with for not working on your exit strategy. When we expect others to take care of our careers at home, often not a lot comes out of it as a result. Why would your international career be different? We have to take the responsibility for the goal and the actions to get to it. Your exit will require as much planning as your initial move. You may also decide to stay in your new home country for good.

Ask yourself some questions early on, regardless if you moved with a permanent or a temporary mindset.

- Where is home? Where does it feel like home?

- Where do you see yourself at the end of the initial assignment?

- When do you need to make a decision about your "next thing"?

- Where will you live in five years?

- Where will you live in ten years?

- Where do you want to retire?

- Where would you live if you had no financial constraints?

- Would you be happy to continue moving around?

- What would stop you from staying abroad?

- What do you need to do to stay in your new location?

- What are the benefits of staying abroad?

- What are the benefits of coming home?

Let's look at a few scenarios to get you thinking about options that you have as your exit or rather your Next Big Thing strategy.

You are an international student. Having paid triple fees at the school of your choice abroad, you are ready to jump into your first big role after graduation. When do you start planning your Next Big Thing? The month of your graduation? Or a little earlier? I hope that you begin thinking about your first job location at least half way through the program. Now, this sounds like a really long time to plan, but it will go by really quickly.

- Start by getting an internship in the location you want to remain in or move to. It's best to work on building relationships that may lead to a permanent job placement in the city where you want to stay. Take an unpaid internship if you have to; it may lead to goodwill and, thus, good connections.

- If you have visa restrictions, understand them really well early on. Are you eligible for a work visa? How long do you have to transfer to a work visa? What other types of visas could you qualify for? Who pays for your visa?

- Network, network, network! Family, friends, fellow students, teachers, colleagues you met during your internship, everyone can potentially help you land your first job. If you need a work visa, network with all the same people, but twice as hard. Let everyone know that you are looking for a job post graduation. Do not be put off by stories about how hard the visas are to obtain. Many other people have managed to get them, why not you?

- Go to every career fair you can find, sponsored by your school, local employers, and entrepreneurial circles.

- Find a local Meetup group in the field close enough to your study and job of interest and go introduce yourself. You will learn something practical and may also meet people who are looking for interns or recent graduates.

- Find local startup incubators and volunteer to do a project for free.

You are an expat on a lucrative two-year assignment. The new location is appealing and you are considering staying. Again, if you haven't breached the topic with your employer and your assignment ends in a month or two, you run the risk of joining that group of disappointed expats. While your employer has invested a lot of money and time into your development as an expat, don't get a sense of false security. No, it's never a 100% guarantee that your employer will want to continue using your talent, time, and dedication despite the investment that has been made so far. Employment at will at home and abroad are not really different concepts. You are responsible for your own destiny and need to figure out what strategy will get you as quickly as possible to the result you expect at the end of your assignment.

The first and most logical thing to do is to talk to your boss about your interest in staying in your host country. If the interest is mutual, great! Now work out the details:

- You have to localize in order to stay. What's the financial impact? Salary, benefits, pension, taxes. Is your job going to be the same or are your responsibilities going to change now that you are not a mercenary but are more vested in building your career locally?

- You can extend your expat contract for another year. Bingo! No change to your finances and another year to think about it. This one still comes with uncertainty. You may have to refer to the point above on localization and make a decision. You are just putting your decision off by a short term that is predefined by your employer.

You have talked to your boss and it's a no go but you are determined to stay in your host country. You just can't imagine living anywhere else next year. Do you need a work visa in order to remain?

- You don't need a visa sponsored by your employer — great. Search for jobs locally as anyone else would. You now have enough experience working in this country and you should have built up some connections to help you with the search.

- You do need a visa to continue working in your dream destination. Your situation is no different from an international student's now. Before you turn to recruiters and to networking events, talk to more people within your company. Very often, while there may be no interest or opportunity with your team, there are plenty of other options. If your boss said it was not going to work out, it might not mean that you will be blocked from trying for other opportunities.

Many expatriate assignments fail. Life abroad can get too hard. You are so much better off because you are taking steps to prepare yourself for what lies ahead. You have spent a significant amount of time researching how to move, fit in, and make the best of it. You will throw yourself into your new life and enjoy the time that you have allocated for the assignment. After all that work, don't waste your exit opportunity! The Next Big Thing can take many forms. What's your next goal? Review alternative scenarios. Think about what type of exit will make you happy and fulfilled. Don't be afraid to think big; what is the most logical outcome may be the simplest. Get through the basics first:

- Are you staying? In what capacity? Staying with the same employer or joining a new business?

- Are you returning to your home country?

- Are you looking for another location to expat to?

Think beyond the geography. You have now augmented your skill set with a new language, the ability to adapt to new cultures, the success management of people or projects internationally, and the ability to make new friends and maintain old relationships successfully. You may be a lot more aware of who you are and what your needs are now than you have ever been. Your needs may have changed and your level of confidence no doubt has gone up dramatically. After all, you are one of the worldly crew now. It's time to take responsibility for achieving your post assignment goals. Perhaps the immediate combination of the best job and the best location isn't there yet. You have worked really hard, hopefully saved some money, and are feeling secure about your immediate future. Consider wild card scenarios and options you may have always wanted to try, or go for something completely new:

- Do you enjoy your job and want to do exactly the same thing but in a new location?

- Should you apply for jobs with a lot more responsibility than you have ever had?

- Do you want to stay in the same industry? Same line of work? Or try something completely different?

- Have you learned new skills that will make you a successful business owner?

- Is it time for a gap year? Focus on discovering what you really want to do for the next five years? Is it going to be an active gap or a vacation?

If you can't decide, then explore various options, as many as time permits. The answer is there somewhere; you just need to keep looking for it. There is no right or wrong exit from your expat assignment, it's up to you to weigh positives and not so positives and decide what fits best as your next move. Whether you choose to repatriate or become a serial expat, I hope that you will feel at home in the destination and life experience that you will choose next.

Chapter 10
Epilogue

Career Mobility = Economic Empowerment of Women

This book was written to consolidate ideas about what makes expats successful through sharing with you international careers and relocation stories of nine women who grew up in different countries and continents, under various political systems, family economic conditions, and beliefs in their own future prospects. We have taken charge of our lives and careers and pursued our dreams around the globe. At the heart of our success were the ingredients of education and career-building skills. We were actively seeking economic independence. We didn't want to rely on others or, perhaps, didn't even have anyone else to support us. What I wanted to share is that it is possible to start with zero, or close to zero, and earn a great living, travel the world, and live in different countries if you focus on being mobile and flexible and keep your options open. I strongly dislike the corporate term of upward mobility. It's someone else defining you and your potential. It makes you want to manage the impressions and perceptions of others. We have defined our own paths, whether they were upward, lateral, or windy as looked upon by other people. We enjoyed every twist and jump around the world.

I wonder what my life would have been like if I remained in Ukraine and continued on a formal and normal path for those who studied English at the university level. A few of my friends have chosen to do that, which means go all the way to PhD programs and most likely continue teaching at the same local university. They are accomplished in their careers, enjoy what they are doing, but are limited in their finances. They are smart people who work really long hours to have a decent local standard of living. The world remains largely closed for them apart from a few vacation opportunities abroad. If they had more chances to immerse into foreign cultures, would that have benefitted their students and themselves? Absolutely. At the same time, I realize that they are doing much better economically than many people with whom they grew up.

Our ability to change jobs, directions, careers, and countries is at the core of expat success. Couple that with the right attitude, never settling, having no fears or barriers, and you get your winning combination. You can go anywhere in the world, make sense out of it, adjust, and fit in.

I didn't want to write this book with only women in mind. The ingredients for expat success are the same for both genders. What I wanted to offer is a perspective that there are plenty of women today who are taking charge of their lives and seeking economic advantages by moving abroad, not as trailing spouses but as leaders, people in charge of their present and future. These women are not afraid of moving to a different continent both to achieve their personal goals and to help their families. On my expat journey I personally met hundreds of women who have done very similar things as I have described in this book. Before I got on the plane for the first time to go to the United States, I had no idea this was the case. These women moved from emerging market economies into more developed countries, and vice versa. I have also met women who are not interested in the private sector but rather are fulfilling their potential through work in nonprofits or academia abroad. All of them either made a decision to move alone or were the ones who facilitated the move of their partners. They took initiative. They came from countries with different levels of women's independence, safety, and income potential. The drive to do better for themselves and their families is what unites their approach to international moves.

What I have also learned is that the idea of "dropping out" of the world of work is not really appealing to them. Women who have resolved to have internationally mobile careers are not interested in confining their lives to homes in whatever country they are based. They may change their priorities, go for a different work–life balance, change their careers, or become entrepreneurs, but they always want to do something that is focused on the world beyond their family unit. They have a lot of energy and experience to share. Reducing the number of hours you commit to your corporate career doesn't mean dropping out. It's simply working out the economics of what can make you happy in any country at any stage of your career. You don't need to run a division or a corporation to be able to say that you are an experienced global professional. If you enjoy an international lifestyle and are doing something meaningful to you, you represent expat success. There are many people who want to do what you have done.

Moving abroad is a risk. At the end of the interviews with my core group featured in this book, I asked the final question: "Knowing everything that you know now about life abroad, would you do it again?" The answer was a resounding yes. The experience has enriched their lives, helped them grow personally and professionally, offered new friendships, increased their career satisfaction and earning potential, and, in some cases, led them to meet their partners or spouses. Some of them, myself including, have become serial expats and continued enjoying the novelty of settling into yet another destination of our mobile lives.

Becoming a Global Citizen

When I first decided to move to the United States, I didn't do any deep reflection on why it was so important for my future. I was fairly young, very ambitious, and had nothing to lose. I had a rather vague idea that an MBA degree could be a way to relative economic freedom. I also very much wanted to travel and experience new places in the United States and beyond. Those were two basic drivers behind the desire to take action and move: make some money and see the world. As simple as that! I wish I could share with you that there was a deeper purpose and meaning behind my decision at that time.

Having moved abroad three times for the past fifteen years and met many women who did the same thing at different times of their lives and career points, I was so fascinated with the similarities of our paths that I had to aggregate the experiences for the benefit of others. This book can help those of you who are at the very start of making your international plans to think further about why you are doing it and what it would take. It also gives you a recipe for becoming a transplant, a successful expat from any level of international experience, be it zero or a high level of experience and sophistication in the matter. Above all, it's about self-discovery and understanding the world beyond our hometowns. It's about becoming global citizens.

What does being a global citizen mean? In Julia's interview she said, "I was a spoilt brat and moving abroad helped me grow up!" I think of her comment as a metaphor of moving from a narrow view on how people, economies, and societies work from the comfort of a small flat, surrounded by those who have exactly the same experience as you, to gradually taking in and processing information from the jungle of the big city, country, and world. It's about understanding that experience goes far beyond knowledge learned from books and TV screens. It's about moving from a comfort zone, breaking routine habits, and no longer being catered to by your family and childhood friends. It's time to have to earn experiences and create connections on your own.

We meet our new friends, co-workers, and potential mates abroad and learn to see beyond the stereotypes. We look for ways to fit in and understand but not change who we are. Moreover, we get interested in different points of view about the same events. We watch multiple news channels, read global blogs, and look for the latest bestselling authors outside of our own countries. We become more flexible and less judgmental. Different doesn't mean wrong, bad, or always painful to get used to. It's what it is — the reality or views that are not the same as we would expect at home. We may even go through phases: we like everything abroad, we hate everything at home; we hate everything abroad, home is just so much better. At some point, a balance is achieved. We learn what we appreciate most at home and in host countries, enjoy the best to its fullest, and cope with the worst.

We get comfortable in international airports: connections are a breeze and we know where the electrical plugs and the favorite shops are. We don't expect the same type of service, interaction, or reaction from locals anymore. We no longer throw tantrums if things don't work the way we expect them to. We still share which country we are from but no longer immediately offer how different or worse things are and how strange we find our new locale. Our accents and idiomatic expressions reflect where we have lived, and it's harder for strangers to identify us with one nation. We struggle to choose just one favorite Olympic team in our iPhone app. We start watching completely alien sports. Passport control officers pick up our passports and say with reverence, "You have travelled a lot!" In many cities we get approached by our home country nationals as well as by locals for directions in multiple languages. We are finally comfortable again with visiting home and sharing our adventures in a way that doesn't sound like bragging. Finally, we listen when the next generation of future global wanderers approach us for advice. We want to mentor and support the audacious international dreams of others like someone did for us years ago. We accept that there are things that our less globally inclined parents will never completely get about our lives.

Our friendships are global — we know there is no way we can have all our favorite people together in the same place, apart from Facebook. We have learned how to cherish relationships and stay connected. We enthusiastically accept the need for video conferencing in our personal and work lives. We choose jobs that allow us to continue on our global lifestyle paths. It's really hard to stop now: not only do we have to continue to work for a living and support the lifestyle that we crave, but also there is so much we can offer as globally minded, international careerists! We don't get oversaturation from our experiences; instead, we continue learning through formal educational programs, corporate training, or our own plans. There are so many more countries to see, we can't stop at this stage! We learn foreign languages to better get into locals' heads and appreciate the blend of their philosophy and way of expression. Successful expats are global citizens. They are comfortable with who they are, how they process the world, and how they are perceived.

To wrap up, I want to emphasize that the stories you have been exposed to are experiences of "women next door" who made their moves abroad and, in retrospect, wished they read something like this book before they did to make the adaptation process just a bit smoother. The goals they had are absolutely achievable and do not require an extreme amount of funding and luck. They do require a great attitude, focus, planning, and a support structure. I hope that our stories inspire you to take the first step toward your international dream, toward moving without shaking!

Acknowledgments

This book would not have been possible without the contributions of eight amazing women who agreed to be interviewed and to share their expat stories. They have supported me through the process of putting the concept together and writing via meetings around the world, Skype sessions, and emails. They have tirelessly read my drafts and provided feedback. They shared truths and emotions of their lives abroad. Aleksandra Romaniuk, Claire Li, Diana Marin, Ekaterina Kalygina, Julia Andrianova-Figg, Karen Strouse, Olga Bokhonovskaya, Sandra Banos, you are my inspiration!

I would also like to thank all the volunteers who read my numerous drafts, discussed the concept in depth, and supported my book and business idea. Christina Heiniger, Elena Bychkovskikh, Leeanne de Wit, Oleg Kulda, Selma Radovac, thank you for being my first readers and supporters! Special thanks to Oleg for pushing me to think about the strategy for the whole venture, not just the book, before I even realized there could be a venture!

I really appreciate the support of all my friends who have tirelessly discussed this book project at the very beginning and stayed with it until the very end of production. Thank you for donating your thoughts and time to this for a whole year: Dan Von Weihe, Daniel Blaettler, Fateh Amroune, Lisa Chaney, Lisa

Ross-Magenty Blaettler, Stacie Saccomanno, Sue Petersen, and Yannick Heiniger.

Thanking Jeff Fadiman for contributions to this book is not saying anything at all. Thank you, Jeff, for getting me started on my international journey and completely changing my life. Thank you for being my mentor and dear friend since the first day we met!

And finally, thank you Martin, my love, for inspiring me to start, pushing me to write, and pressuring me to finish. You have read and reread every paragraph, commented on style, content, and tone better than any professional editor ever would. You have made me believe that it's a story worth telling and that I can become a writer. So here it is, my first book, dedicated to you!

Bibliography

Taleb, Nassim Nicholas. *Antifragile*. London: Penguin, 2012.

L'Auberge Espagnole, 2002. Film. Directed by Cédric Klapisch. France-Spain: Bac Films, Ce Qui Me Meut Motion Pictures, France 2 Cinéma, Mate Films, Mate Producciones S.A., Studio Canal, Via Digital.

Les Poupeés Russes, 2005. Film. Directed by Cédric Klapisch. France-United Kingdom: Lunar Films, StudioCanal, France 2 (FR2), Canal +, Ce Qui Me Meut Motion Pictures, TPS Cinema.

Gladwell, Malcolm. *Outliers: The Story of Success*. New York: Little, Brown, 2008.

Stephen Fear Interview with BizBritain, 2012

http://www.youtube.com/watch?v=vOBzNp9N-LY

Edmund S. Muskie Graduate Fellowship Program
http://www.irex.org/project/edmund-s-muskie-graduate-fellowship-program

Roger Riddell. *Short on funding? Try these 5 education crowdfunding options*. 2013.
http://www.educationdive.com/news/short-on-funding-try-these-5-education-crowdfunding-options/167854/

The World Is Not Enough,1999. Film. Directed by Michael Apted, UK: Danjaq, Eon Productions, Metro-Goldwyn-Mayer (MGM), United Artists.

Weiner, Eric. *The Geography of Bliss.* New York: Grand Central Publishing, 2008.

Cinderella Man, 2005. Film. Directed by Ron Howard. U.S.: Universal Pictures, Miramax Films, Imagine Entertainment, Parkway Productions.

Burns, Judith. *"Alarming shortage" of foreign language skills in UK.* 2013.
http://www.bbc.co.uk/news/education-25003828

"The lottery of life. Where to be born in 2013." *The Economist,* 2012.
http://www.economist.com/news/21566430-where-be-born-2013-lottery-life

Lewis, Michael. *Boomerang: The Biggest Bust.* London: Penguin, 2012.

Safian, Robert. *This is generation flux: meet the pioneers of the new (and chaotic) frontier of business.* 2012.
http://www.fastcompany.com/1802732/generation-flux-meet-pioneers-new-and-chaotic-frontier-business

Hewlett, Sylvia Ann and Rashid, Ripa. *Winning the War for Talent in Emerging Markets: Why Women Are the Solution.* Boston: Harvard Business School Press, 2011.

About the Author

Yelena Parker is a career expatriate and an executive coach. Born in Ukraine, she has worked in twenty countries, travelled through twenty six, and lived in the United States, Switzerland, and the United Kingdom, where she is now based. She has a Postgraduate Diploma in Strategy and Innovation from Oxford University, Saïd Business School, and an MBA from San Jose State University in California. She has over ten years of international business experience working with a wide swathe of American technology companies including Cisco, Verisign, and Symantec. Parker founded her executive coaching consultancy, Moving Without Shaking Ltd., to help people achieve their dreams of living a truly global life. Visit http://movingwithoutshaking.com. Follow her on Twitter @yelenaparker and @movingwtshaking